Stefan Buczacki

Best Garden Doctor

HAMLYN

Publishing Director Laura Bamford
Design Manager Bryan Dunn
Designer Tony Truscott
Executive Editor Julian Brown
Editor Meg Sanders
Assistant Editor Karen O'Grady
Production Josephine Allum
Picture Research Jenny Faithfull

First published in Great Britain in 1997
by Hamlyn
an imprint of Reed International Books Limited
Michelin House, 81 Fulham Road, London SW3 6RB
and Auckland, Melbourne, Singapore and Toronto

Reprinted 1998

Produced by Toppan Printing Co.(H.K) Ltd.
Printed in Hong Kong

ISBN 0 600 59754 7

A catalogue of this book is available at the British Library

CONTENTS

INTRODUCTION

"Plants, like people and animals, are living things and, like all other living things, they may fall ill. Sometimes, there's very little that we can do to prevent this, but taking good care of the plants we grow is a very good start. For, other things being equal, like people and animals, plants will only grow and remain in good health if they are properly looked after. Neglect and unhygienic practices will lead to disease and pest infestation in the garden, just as in the home.

I strongly believe that pest and disease control shouldn't be a haphazard operation and that you shouldn't rely solely on the advice on the packet or chemical bottle. Before attempting to prevent or control a problem, it makes sense to try and appreciate the nature of the cause and to know your enemy. With this knowledge, you will be in a much better position to choose remedial or avoiding action and to appreciate why other, apparently sensible courses of action will not, in practice, have any effect. I want you to enjoy your garden and your plants. I want you to do that by keeping them as healthy as possible. But I also want you to realise that some damage is tolerable and that knowledge of garden plant problems can itself be a quite fascinating subject. I hope therefore that this book will lead you towards more enjoyment of your gardening through enabling you to keep matters in perspective, to control those that need controlling and not to develop hypochondria about those that don't."

The causes of garden problems

PESTS

A plant pest is an animal that causes a plant to malfunction. Pests are an enormous and diverse group of creatures that represent most of the main types of animal. They range in size from microscopic eelworms to red deer and, unlike the organisms that cause diseases, the advantage with pests is that it's often possible to see your enemy, if not always to look him in the eye. With such a wide range of animal types, it's incredibly difficult to generalise over the way they cause damage. Nonetheless, it is possible to make a broad division into sucking creatures and chewing creatures, the latter group including beetles, caterpillars and squirrels, while the former includes pests such as aphids, whiteflies and, appropriately enough, insects called suckers.

While chewing pests can quickly cause a considerable amount of damage, it is the size of the initial population that is the governing factor. So, although one rabbit can create a great deal of havoc, one caterpillar, which will be unable to multiply on the plant, may ultimately cause a fairly small amount of damage, even if it's allowed to continue unchecked. With many of the sucking pests, however, it is the adult form that is often the active creature and will reproduce and multiply on the plant; miss the first few aphids of the season and there will very soon be hundreds, if not thousands of individuals to contend with.

Most of us will never see an eelworm, here magnified one hundred times

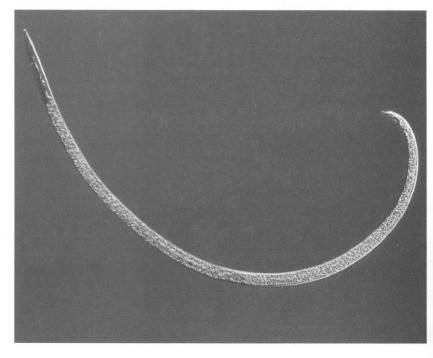

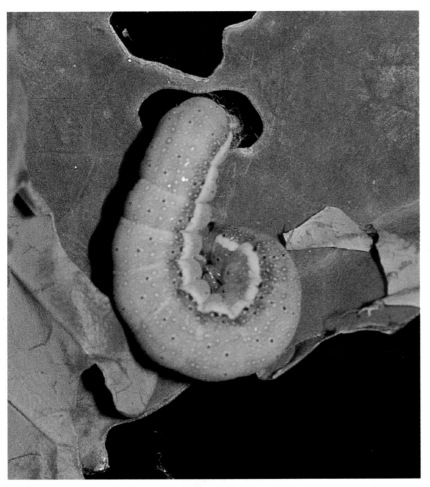

As with all other aspects of garden plant health however, we must keep matters in proportion. Although most groups of the animal kingdom include some pest species, they are usually but relatively small fractions of the total. Among around one hundred British species of slug and snail for instance, only eight cause a serious nuisance in gardens and even among some five hundred species of aphid, only about seventy five affect garden plants to a significant extent. Wholesale destruction of any form of animal life is never remotely justifiable therefore.

Caterpillars and sawfly larvae are typical chewing pests

Although I've said that pest species occur among many of the groups of the animal kingdom, there's no doubt that one group, the insects, outweighs all others in importance. More pests occur among the insects than among all other groups put together and they include aphids, beetles, caterpillars of butterflies and moths, whiteflies, thrips and leafhoppers among many others. Most reproduce by laying eggs and passing through an immature or larval form, which is very often the stage in which they cause most damage to our plants.

In some instances, both adults and larvae are troublesome, while the rapidly multiplying aphids referred to earlier achieve their population explosions by, rather surprisingly, giving birth to living young. Other invert-ebrate pests are found among woodlice, millepedes, slugs and snails (molluscs) and microscopic eelworms. At the other end of the spectrum lie birds and, of course, a considerable number of mammals ranging in size from voles and mice, through moles and rabbits to deer.

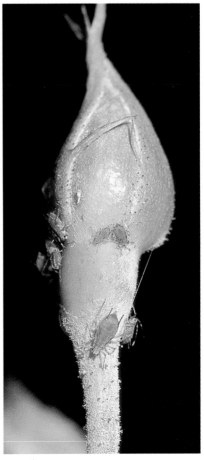

Aphids multiply very rapidly

DISEASES

A disease is an affliction of a garden plant caused by an organism other than an animal. In practice, this means a fungus, a bacterium, or something mysterious and sub-microscopic, generally a virus. Although these three groups of organisms are quite unrelated to each other, they do have some features in common. None of them possess the green colouring matter, chlorophyll. So although they aren't animals, neither are they plants, which use chlorophyll to manufacture their own food substances from the raw materials of carbon dioxide and water. Fungi, bacteria and viruses must, therefore, feed differently and they do this by growing on the organic materials contained in other living things.

Those fungi and bacteria that feed solely on dead matter are called saprobes and those that feed on still-living matter have the more familiar

One common symptom of bacterial attack is soft rot, as on these swedes

name, parasites. When a parasite causes a disease, it's called a pathogen and the plant that is attacked is called its 'host'. Fungi and bacteria that live

parasitically are my main concern in this book, but it should be remembered that there are hundreds of saprobic species of vital importance in the garden, for they are the means by which compost and other organic remains are broken down so that the chemicals contained in them can be returned to the soil as plant food. The heat that's generated in a well-built compost heap is the result of the chemical processes for which these saprobes are responsible.

Don't imagine that the division into saprobe and parasite is water-tight. Many fungi and bacteria are capable of living in both states: a Jekyll and Hyde existence. The simple fact that some pathogens can live in innocuous fashion on dead organic matter and then turn their attention to living tissue under-lines the importance of garden hygiene that I discuss on page 10. *Botrytis* grey mould is a very important example of

By contrast, fungus on these swedes has produced fluffy mould growth

this and is as much at home on piles of dead vegetation as it is on living plants. By contrast, there are some fungi and bacteria that can only survive on a living plant; rusts and mildews are all too familiar examples of this group.

Fungi can be seen *en masse* in the form of mould or as distinct individuals in the form of toadstools, for example. Even bacteria, which individually are microscopic, can often be seen as coloured droplets, each containing millions of separate cells. Viruses are quite different. They are all highly specialised and can exist only within the living cells of another organism with which they form a very close, parasitic relationship. They are, therefore, quite invisible to the naked eye and, indeed, quite invisible with a normal microscope. Complex and powerful electron microscopes, capable of magnifying many hundreds of thousands of times are needed to reveal them.

Most of the important diseases of people are caused by viruses, with bacteria a close second and fungi a fairly insignificant third. The reverse tends to be true with plants, however, and most of the diseases described in this book are caused by fungi. In order to understand some of the control measures outlined in the following pages, it's important to appreciate two features of the life history and biology of fungi.

They are very likely to be damaged by drying out and are, by and large, unable to grow and feed at low temperatures; for example, during winter in temperate climates. This problem is compounded for parasites by the fact that their host plant has very probably died down to survive only as a

rootstock, corm or seed. During the winter, therefore, fungi are in a vulnerable condition and unable to spread and disperse rapidly. In summer, however, they are able to multiply and disperse very rapidly indeed because their method of reproduction produces not seeds, but spores; much smaller,

relatively fragile bodies that are easily blown by the wind to new hosts, where they then proceed to germinate and grow into new organisms extremely quickly. Much of plant disease control and avoidance is directed towards preventing the formation and dispersal of these spores.

Viruses are invisible but are often betrayed by distinctive leaf patterns

CULTURAL AND PHYSICAL REMEDIES

"Healthy gardens don't happen by accident. They are usually the result of a combination of factors: sound and sensible horticultural practice, the way that the garden has been managed in the previous and earlier seasons, the soil and site conditions, the weather in any particular season, a fair measure of good luck and, possibly, some form of chemical or biological pest and disease control. It's not easy for a gardener to do much more than influence the first and last of these categories. The question of chemical control is discussed on page 16 and biological control on page 12. Here I shall outline the ways in which good gardening practice, aided by the purely physical technique of the trapping of pests can have a major impact on plant health."

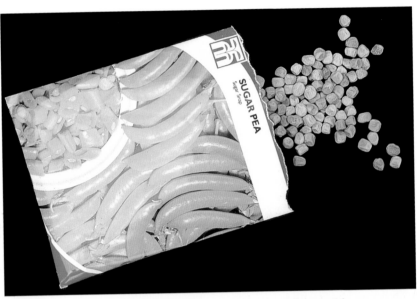

Packeted seeds are of very high quality and without any disease risk

Prevention is better than cure

Prevention is not only better, it's also cheaper than cure if that cure has to be a direct control measure. Pest and disease prevention can be carried in two ways: through the plant itself and through the garden environment in which the plant will be grown. When establishing a new planting, therefore, it's essential to obtain your plants, seeds, bulbs or other planting material from a reputable supplier, because pests and diseases of one type or another can be carried on any of them.

Newly purchased plants in the form of transplant-sized individuals, crowns, rootstocks or young trees or shrubs should be inspected carefully and any

Planting bulbs on a layer of sand will help to prevent rotting

obviously damaged or diseased parts immediately cut away.

Seeds don't normally show visible signs of any diseases that they may be carrying, but a reputable supplier will always find it in his interest to ensure that his seed stock is derived from healthy plants and that it has been prepared for packeting in as clean and careful a way as possible. It's highly improbable that, these days, in this country, you will find particles of soil or plant debris with the seed in a packet. Nonetheless, a great number of gardeners save their own seed; and I would encourage them to do so as it is highly satisfying, but it is important to try and emulate commercial quality standards and, above all, only save seed from plants that are themselves vigorous and healthy.

It's perhaps in the area of ornamental bulbs that most problems are encountered. The sale of 'job lots' of decidedly inferior quality daffodil and narcissus bulbs is something that regrettably, still continues. Close examination of these bulbs will reveal, not only that many are undersized compared with those from a well-known and reputable source, but that many have small surface lesions, indicative of a disease problem and sometimes scarring or erosion of the surface, as evidence of pest attack. When you lift bulbs from your own garden, you should sort out or, to use the correct term, 'rogue' the stock and throw away any showing signs of disease. It may seem wasteful at the time, but viewed against the likelihood of introducing contamination into an entire bed, it is a sound insurance policy. And, with bulbs and corms, the insurance policy might well extend to the routine use of a fungicide dip on those to be retained.

Where seeds or bulbs, corms and tubers have been collected or lifted from the garden, there's a further factor to be considered, for while they may be perfectly healthy at the time of lifting, they can deteriorate during storage. Cool, dry, well-ventilated conditions are needed for bulbs, combined with a dusting using one of the combined fungicide and insecticide dressings now available. Seeds are best stored in paper packets in a fridge, ideally within a screw-top glass jar with a sachet of moisture-absorbing silica gel, available from pharmacists.

Vegetatively propagated plants are most at risk from virus contamination

Viruses and plants

There is one group of diseases for which purchasing healthy stock is the essential prevention: these are the diseases caused by viruses. The crops affected most seriously are those that are propagated vegetatively; that is by cuttings, bulbs, corms, tubers and the like, rather than seeds. This is because any virus contamination is likely to be present throughout the plants' tissues and is thus passed on from parent to off-spring. (Rather few viruses can be carried in the seed.) An individual gardener can't do anything to rid any already-contaminated plants of virus and this is one reason why 'seed' tubers of potatoes are best not saved from the garden but bought afresh each season, and why plants that are bought in such as dahlias, carnations and chrysanthemums should be examined carefully before they are used for new plantings. With longer-term crops such as fruit bushes and trees, ensuring that healthy stock is obtained is even more important. Always buy only certified virus-free plants.

Modern antirrhinum varieties have some resistance to rust disease

Resistance to pests and diseases

You will sometimes hear of plants that have an inbuilt resistance to pests and diseases and must wonder why these aren't more widely available. The problem is that plant breeders can only make use of resistance that occurs naturally in wild plants. Where these are significantly different from the cultivated forms, it may be impossible to breed the resistance into the cultivated plants without losing some other desirable features. And because the process will, in any event, be long and costly, it is only really worthwhile with major commercial crops, such as cereals. Where resistance does exist and is of use to gardeners, I mention it; but this isn't often.

Woodlice may indicate untidiness

A tidy garden is a healthy garden

Pests and diseases don't materialise from thin air, although they sometimes seem to arrive in the garden as if by magic during the early part of the summer. Some may have been brought in on plants, but it's the garden, the neighbouring gardens and surrounding area that are likely to be the source of many more. Although you can't do much to influence events beyond the boundary, a great deal can be achieved within your own garden.

First, there's the simple matter of tidiness, for a neat and tidy garden is much more likely to be healthy than one that is cluttered with rubbish, debris and the remains of old plants.

The fact that certain pathogens can live both in saprobic and parasitic states is one obvious reason for this cleanliness, but even those pathogens that only exist on living plants are very rarely so specialised in their diet that they can survive only on one particular plant species. Usually, they can live equally well on a range of types, including many garden weeds, so a weedy garden is quite likely to be harbouring pathogens and, probably, many pests too.

But please don't, in the cause of garden hygiene, clear away all natural vegetation. A balance is needed, for the simple reason that removing all 'undesirable' vegetation will probably achieve the same result as the widespread removal of hedgerows in the countryside at large: the habitats of the natural enemies of many pest and disease organisms have been removed. This means that the very ones that we want to control are left free to multiply.

Physical pest control

Although not relevant to garden diseases, the use of traps can be invaluable in pest control. At their simplest, these are barriers: netting over soft fruit to keep out birds, lightweight fleece over vegetables to protect them from egg-laying flies or caterpillars, or prickly twigs around soft plants to deter slugs. At a slightly more sophisticated level, they can take the form of sticky cards to enmesh whiteflies, while at their most advanced, they can be pheromone baited devices to lure fruit moths to their fate.

Shredders help ensure that almost all waste matter can be composted

BIOLOGICAL REMEDIES

"I'm often asked what has changed most in gardening since I began my horticultural career many years ago. I've had different answers at different times, generally relating to trends in the types of plants most favoured. Over recent seasons, however, my answer has unequivo- cally been the greater use of biological pest control. The use of natural parasites and predators to control pests certainly isn't new. Farmers in China were doing it in the thirteenth century by putting ants into their litchi and citrus trees to protect them from pest attack; in modern times, it has been used with success in commercial horticulture and agriculture.

At the end of the nineteenth century, for instance, a predaceous Australian species of ladybird was introduced into California to control a serious insect pest of citrus orchards. Much more recently, the use of parasites and predators has been very valuable in the control of pests in greenhouses, where the restricted environment is particularly favourable for their use: the greenhouse being enclosed, the predators are unlikely to fly away and, being warm, there is no incentive for them to venture outside. Only over the past few years, however, have production, marketing and packaging methods been developed to make some biological control methods available to amateur gardeners. Although they may still be fairly expensive and not always easy to apply effectively, there's no doubt that their use will certainly spread."

Encouraging natural biological control

Because a number of biological control methods are now available to gardeners, there's a tendency to forget that comparable phenomena already occur and operate naturally in gardens. You can do a good deal towards helping pest control by encouraging these natural systems. Among many groups of beneficial garden insects are various species of ground beetle, hoverflies, lacewings, ladybirds and many groups of flies among which the

Wasps are annoying but are valuable in feeding on many garden pests

Both adult and larval ladybirds feed on aphids and keep them in check

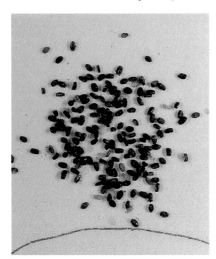

Whitefly control, sold on cards

Biological control analysed

ADVANTAGES

■ No chemicals of any type are involved, a boon for gardeners who eschew the use of chemicals.

■ The methods are natural in that they make use of a preference that a creature displays in the wild, although not necessarily in the same country.

■ The treatments are often fairly specific because a particular control agent will affect only a particular pest or group of pests. This is rarely the case with chemicals.

■ There is no possibility of damage being caused to the plants such as may occur when chemicals are used; some plant species, for instance, may be susceptible to scorching brought about by the action of chemicals and, in hot weather, even resilient plants may sometimes be affected adversely.

DISADVANTAGES

■ The methods are relatively expensive compared with most chemical controls.

■ Few methods are suitable for use outdoors.

■ No chemicals or general traps (such as sticky yellow cards) may be used to control other pests affecting the same plants as these will also kill the predators.

ichneumonids, that parasitise caterpillars, are the best known. Try to keep garden pesticide use to a minimum so as not to harm these creatures and, in particular, avoid the use of chemicals that persist in the environment for some time. Quite understandably, gardeners tend to use pesticides most when they see the most pests. In reality, the bulk of the damage to the plants may by then already have been done and the pest populations could be about to collapse as predators build up. By using pesticides at that stage, you may be doing more harm than good.

■ In small greenhouses, such as those in most gardens, the predator or parasite may rapidly eliminate the pest and then itself die out. Repeat applications (and therefore repeat purchases) may be necessary. In commercial greenhouses, there will always be sufficient pests remaining for the predator to continue.

■ It may be necessary to predict the occurrence of a pest problem some time in advance because few control agents are available off the shelf; they must be ordered from the suppliers.

■ There are no biological control methods available for gardeners to use against plant diseases.

Notes on biological controls

■ The ways in which the different methods act vary. The bacterial spray for caterpillars and also the nematode based controls all depend on bacteria to attack and degrade the target pest, so bringing about its death. The parasitic wasps and gall midges act by laying their eggs into the pest. These then hatch and the resulting larvae do the rest; not pleasant to contemplate perhaps but effective and certainly natural. The ladybird beetle, both in larval and adult form feeds wholesale on mealy bugs.

■ The recommended minimum temperatures vary slightly between the companies marketing the controls but, within defined limits, all work better as the temperature rises.

■ Always check the directions carefully with regard to the method of application and for details of how long and under what conditions the organisms will remain effective after you receive them.

■ Finally, it should be added that none of these biological control organisms is in any way harmful to humans. In the case of the bacterial spray, the bacteria themselves are in a liquid suspension and in this form are sprayed directly onto the target caterpillars. The nematodes, contrary to what is often supposed, do not themselves kill pests but penetrate their bodies and so introduce bacteria which in turn bring about the pest's death.

Biological control methods available for garden use

Pest	Biological control organism	Notes
Aphids	*Aphidoletes aphidimyza* [predatory gall midge]	Greenhouse; min air temp 10°C (50°F)
Aphids	*Aphidius matricariae* [predatory gall midge]	Greenhouse; min air temp 18°C (65°F)
Caterpillars	*Bacillus thuringiensis* [bacterium]	Greenhouse/outdoors; applied as a spray
Mealy bug	*Cryptoleamus montrouzieri* [ladybird beetle]	Greenhouse; min air temp 20°C (68°F)
Red spider mites	*Phytoseiulus persimilis* [predatory mite]	Best in greenhouse; min air temp 16°C (61°F)
Scale insects (soft scale only)	*Metaphycus helvolus* [parasitic wasp]	Greenhouse; min air temp 22°C (72°F)
Slugs	*Phasmarhabditis hermaphroditica* [nematode carrying bacteria]	Outdoors; min soil temp 5°C (41°F)
Soil pests (some)	*Steinernema carpocapsae* [nematode carrying bacteria]	Outdoors; min soil temp 14°C (58°F)
Vine weevil (larvae)	*Heterorhabditis megadis* [nematode carrying bacteria]	Outdoors; min soil temp 12°C (54°F)
Vine weevil (larvae)	*Steinernema carpocapsae* [nematode carrying bacteria]	Outdoors; min soil temp 14°C (58°F)
Whiteflies	*Encarsia formosa* [parasitic wasp]	Greenhouse; min air temp 18°C (65°F)

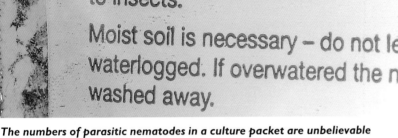

This sachet contains 3 million live nematodes (*Heterorhabditis megidis*) in moist clay. Each nematode carries a bacterium specific to insects.

Moist soil is necessary – do not let waterlogged. If overwatered the ne washed away.

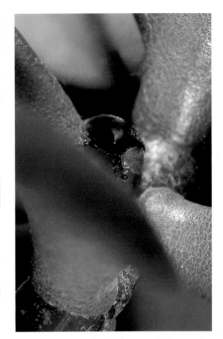

The numbers of parasitic nematodes in a culture packet are unbelievable

Cryptoleamus feeds on mealy bugs

Spiders are among the most important creatures aiding pest control

CHEMICAL REMEDIES

"It's a sad commentary on life that something from a bottle or a packet has become the first answer to so many of our needs or problems. Modern medicine, with numerous drugs and remedies freely prescribed or on sale over the counter is just a part of this trend. As so many people reach for a chemical answer to their own ailments, it's small wonder that they apply the same principles to their gardens and drench the first sign of the smallest blemish with one of the dozens of sprays now available. This isn't, can't be, the correct approach; yet I don't believe that rejecting chemicals entirely is any better.

The worst of both worlds is to adopt the attitude that chemicals are acceptable only if they are of natural, rather than factory origin. Some of the most noxious of chemicals (digitalis, cocaine, strychnine) originate in plants and some of the products supported so enthusiastically by many 'green' gardeners have far-reaching effects. For instance, derris (rotenone), a natural product, is highly toxic to fish, whereas pirimicarb, a synthetic one, is selectively toxic to aphids and little else.

In my advice on these pages, therefore, I've tried to adopt a median approach that, I hope, reflects common sense. And just because a chemical occurs naturally in the environment in a harmless and dilute form is no guarantee that the same chemical, made up as a concentrate to use as a garden spray will still be similarly innocuous to the environment."

Use of chemicals

The chemicals on sale through garden centres and shops must, by law, have been cleared for use by the Ministry of Agriculture. The Ministry will have been satisfied that thorough evidence has demonstrated both the effectiveness and the safety of a product, when used for the purpose described and in the manner directed. The last phrase is the key one, for almost anything, including pepper and salt from your kitchen, can cause harm if over used or used in an unconventional way. Most of us know enough about pepper and salt to realise what is right and what is wrong. Very few of us, however, know enough about garden chemicals to make such judgements and the guidance of the

manufacturers as given on the product labels must be adhered to strictly.

It's most important only to use chemicals sold specifically for garden use. You mustn't use household chemicals in the garden as these can be very hazardous when they are not being used for their intended purpose. And nor should you turn, for your supply, to commercial plant-growers and farmers. They use far greater quantities of a far greater range of products than any gardener, and apply quite different criteria since they operate in commercial situations. This difference in product range may be due simply to marketing considerations; a particular chemical may not be worth selling in very small quantities. In recent seasons, this has become apparent as fewer and fewer chemicals remain

Broad bean rust can be controlled by using the right type of fungicide

available to gardeners because chemical companies cannot afford the very high costs of the regular re-registrations that are required. But certain chemicals are restricted for use in the commercial market because their application may need techniques or precautions that are accessible only to the commercial operator; the product itself may not be intrinsically any more hazardous.

INSECTICIDES AND FUNGICIDES

Insecticides are chemicals intended to kill insects, whereas fungicides are chemicals intended to kill fungi. But the spectrum of pest and disease-causing species extends, of course, beyond insects and fungi, so what is to be done about bacteria and viruses, invertebrates other than insects, and, indeed, birds and mammals. Most insecticides will have some effect on other living creatures, which is why we have to take precautions when handling them. Many insecticides will have some controlling effect on pests such as woodlice and millepedes but almost none will have any impact on mites, eelworms, slugs and snails. These last two pests are combated with specific molluscicides, of which two are available to gardeners. Some fungicides will control bacteria but not very efficiently; specific bacteria controlling chemicals (antibiotics) are generally banned from any horticultural use because of the likelihood of bacteria that causes human ailments being exposed to them and perhaps developing resistance or tolerance. No chemical will have any direct effect on viruses but the spread of viruses can be lessened by controlling the aphids or other creatures which introduce them into plant tissue.

No chemical will have any effect on rose mosaic or other virus diseases

Red spider mites are unaffected by most insecticides, but dislike water

CHEMICAL REMEDIES

Choice of chemicals

If you walk into a garden centre or garden shop, you will see a very large display of both insecticides and fungicides on sale. How do you make a choice from the many that are available? When trying to make your decision, you should appreciate that there is actually only a limited number of chemical ingredients and the same substances are sold under several different brand names. Most advice offered in books, leaflets and on radio and television refers to the chemical, not their brand names. I've adopted the same principle in this book, so to find a specific product, you should look for the chemical name or 'active ingredient' on the product label. It will generally be in smaller sized print than the brand name but it must, by law, be there.

It's important to understand that not all fungicides or insecticides will control all types of disease or pest with equal efficiency. Unless you have a very serious problem with one specific or unusual pest or disease, and must therefore use a very specific chemical, try to buy those products that will treat a wide range of problems and which are said to have a broad spectrum of effectiveness. Many products contain a blend of chemicals to enhance this spectrum; some proprietary rose treatments, for instance, include both a fungicide to control mildew, black spot and rust, and an insecticide to combat aphids. You must not, however, mix together two different products yourself unless the manufacturers state specifically that this is permissible. You may reduce the overall effectiveness and/or damage your plants. And do check also that your chosen product may safely be used on your particular plant. Some plants (ferns and fuchsias are common examples) may be harmed by products, even those based on natural soaps, that are otherwise perfectly safe.

Systemic and non-systemic compounds

You will often see the word systemic on packaging of garden chemicals. A systemic chemical is one that is absorbed by the plant and moved in the sap from one part of the plant to another. By contrast, a non-systemic or contact product remains on the surface of the plant and kills pathogen or pest as the two come into direct contact there. There are advantages and disadvantages with both. The systemic product is required in smaller quantities, can be sprayed with much less accuracy (the plant itself ensures uniform distribution within), is not liable to be washed off by rain, which would diminish its effectiveness, and is able to penetrate and eradicate pests or pathogens that are concealed and protected from more direct action. There are, nonetheless, disadvantages with edible produce, for the fact that systemic chemicals are taken up into the plant's tissues and have a long-lasting effect means also that the safe interval between the time of application and the time that the produce may be eaten is correspondingly longer. In the kitchen garden, therefore, a contact chemical is often the better choice. At the present time, the principle systemic chemicals still available for garden use are fungicides, most or all of the insecticides having been phased out, although many are used commercially. Although fungicidal chemicals have less impact in general on the environment than insecticides, all chemicals should be treated with respect.

Leaf miners are beyond the effect of contact insecticides

Safe use of garden chemicals

The single most important precaution is to read the label carefully and use the product only in the way and for the purpose described. But there are other considerations too, some a simple matter of common sense:

■ Don't use any chemicals that have lost their labels and don't decant chemicals from a large pack into a smaller one. Garden chemicals must only be kept in their original packaging.

■ Don't mix or prepare garden chemicals in the kitchen, and keep easily identified sprayers, watering cans or other equipment specifically for pest

Care must always be taken to avoid harm to bees when using insecticides

and disease control. Don't use the same equipment for fertilizers or weedkillers.

■ Wash out equipment thoroughly after use and pour excess diluted product on to an area of waste ground. Waste concentrated products should be disposed of according to the advice offered by your local authority.

■ Store all chemicals out of reach of children and pets, preferably in a locked cupboard and away from extremes of temperature.

■ Don't spray plants in strong wind, in bright sunlight or when flowers are fully open. The chemicals may damage flowers and cause harm to pollinating insects. The best times for application are the early morning or late evening when bees are fairly inactive.

A good crop of garden fruit needn't depend on using chemical sprays

Chemicals available for garden pest and disease control

Fungicides (chemicals to control diseases)

Chemical	Mode of action	Note	Uses
Ammonium carbonate	Contact	Only in mixture with copper sulphate	See copper sulphate
Ammonium hydroxide	Contact	Only in mixture with copper sulphate	See copper sulphate
Bupirimate	Systemic	Only in mixture with triforine	See triforine
Captan	Contact	Only in hormone rooting powder	To protect cuttings from rotting
Carbendazim	Systemic	The most widely used fungicide, taking the place of the now withdrawn benomyl	A very wide range of diseases of edible and ornamental plants and lawns
Copper oxychloride	Contact		See copper sulphate
Copper sulphate	Contact	Only in mixture with ammonium hydroxide as Bordeaux Mixture and ammonium carbonate as Cheshunt Compound	A wide range of diseases on edible and ornamental plants. Especially useful against blight and rust
Dichlorophen	Contact	As a fungicide, only in hormone rooting powder. (But also widely used as a moss killer)	To protect cuttings from rotting
Mancozeb	Contact		Especially useful against blight and rusts
Myclobutanil	Systemic		Especially against rose diseases and apple scab
Penconazole	Contact		Especially against rust diseases on ornamental plants
Sulphur	Contact	Alone as liquid or powder and also in combination with other chemicals	Especially useful against mildew and as protection for stored ornamental bulbs
Thiophanate-methyl	Systemic	As a root dip formulation for brassica transplants	Only for clubroot control
Triforine	Systemic	Only in mixtures, either with bupirimate or with sulphur and insecticide	Especially for rose diseases; also fruit but not vegetables

Insecticides (chemicals to control pests, especially insects)

Chemical	Mode of action	Notes	Uses
Bendiocarb	Contact/systemic		To control ants and other crawling insects
Bifenthrin	Contact		Most pests on edible and ornamental plants
Bioallethrin	Contact	Only in mixture with permethrin	See permethrin
Borax	Contact		As ant bait

Chlorpyrifos	Contact		To control ants and other crawling insects
Cypermethrln	Contact		To control ants and other crawling insects
Deltamethrin	Contact		To control ants and other crawling insects
Fenitrothion	Contact		
Heptenophos	Contact	Only in mixture with permethrin	See permethrin
Horticultural soaps (natural fatty acids)	Contact		Aphids, whiteflies, red spider mites and soft scale on edible and ornamental plants
Lindane	Contact		To control soil pests
Malathion	Contact	Alone and in mixture with permethrin	A wide range of pests, especially sap-sucking types on edible and ornamental plants
Permethrin	Contact	The most widely used modern insecticide; alone and in mixtures with other chemicals. Also available as smoke formulation for greenhouse whitefly control	Most pests on edible and garden ornamental plants
Piperonyl butoxide	Contact	Only in mixture with permethrin	A wide range of pests on edible and ornamental plants
Pirimicarb	Contact	Available alone and in mixture with fungicides	Almost specific to aphids
Pyrethrins	Contact	General name for a group of chemically similar substances	See permethrin
Pyrethrum	Contact		A wide range of pests on edible and ornamental plants
Quassia	Contact	Only in mixture with rotenone	See rotenone
Resmethrin	Contact	Only in combination with pyrethrins	See permethrin
Rotenone (derris)	Contact	As liquid or powder, also in combination with quassia	A wide range of pests on edible and ornamental plants
Tar oils	Contact		Control of overwintering pests on deciduous trees and shrubs in the dormant season
Tetramethrin	Contact	Only in mixture with permethrin	See permethrin

Molluscicides (chemicals to control slugs and snails)

Chemical	Mode of action	Notes	Uses
Metaldehyde	Anaesthetic	As liquid and pellets	Slugs and snails
Methiocarb	Gastric action	Only as pellets	Slugs and snails

TROUBLE-SHOOTING CHARTS

"Identification is the key to the successful treatment of any garden problem and there are several ways in which you can approach this. Do bear in mind, nonetheless, that this book can only cover a selection of the many problems that occur in gardens. I've selected those you are most likely to see, but in some seasons, in some areas and especially on less common types of plant, you may see others.

One approach to identifying a particular garden problem is to turn to the section of the book covering the group of plants with which you are concerned, then read and check the illustrations to see if your problem matches any of those that I've described. A second way is to use the index, where all the common plants are listed together with their problems covered in the book; if you already know what the problem is, this is obviously a quicker method. Even if you aren't sure, the name of the pest or disease will sometimes be sufficiently descriptive to give you a clue. Alternatively, you could check through all the problems relating to your particular plant. The third, and most logical way is to use the Trouble-shooting Charts, below. They can't, of course, direct you to the specific problem for your specific plant; that would take many more pages. What they are intended for, however, is to guide you to the type of problem: mildew, aphids and so forth, that your plant may have. Cross-reference to the index should then indicate whether that particular problem occurs commonly on your particular plant. "

	Symptoms on LEAVES	
Problem	**Detail**	**Probable cause**
1. Wilting	General	Short of water
		Root pest or disease
		Wilt disease
2. Holed	Generally ragged	Small pests (millepedes, flea beetles, woodlice)
		Capsid bugs
	Elongate holes; usually with slime present	Slugs or snails
	Fairly large holes, over entire leaf or confined to edges	Caterpillars
		Beetles
	Semi-circular pieces taken from edges	Leaf-cutter bees
3. Discoloured	Black	Sooty mould
	Predominantly red	Short of water
	More or less bleached	Nutrient deficiency
		Short of water
		Too much water
	Silvery (plums)	Silver leaf
	Irregular yellowish patterns	Virus

Problem	Detail	Probable cause
	Irregular tunnels	Leaf miners
	Surface flecking	Leafhoppers
	Various (tomatoes)	See page 66
	Brown (scorched) in spring	Frost
4. Spotted	Brownish, angular, with mould beneath	Downy mildew
	Brownish, irregular or rounded; no mould	Leaf spot
	Dark brown or black; not dusty	Scab
	Small, dusty, brown, black or brightly coloured	Rust
5. Mouldy	Black	Sooty mould
	Grey, fluffy	Grey mould
	White, velvety	Mildew
	Brown (tomatoes)	Leaf mould
	White, beneath leaves (potatoes)	Blight
6. Infested with insects	White, moth-like, tiny	Whiteflies
	Green, grey, black or other colour	Aphids
	White, woolly (greenhouse)	Mealy bugs
	Flat, encrusted, like limpets	Scale insects
	Large, six legs, worm-like	Caterpillars
7. Curling	Insects present also	See 6
	Tightly rolled in spring (roses)	Sawflies
	Puckered, reddish (peaches and almonds)	Peach leaf curl
	Puckered, yellowish (pears)	Pear leaf blister mites
8. Cobwebs present	Plant wilting	Red spider mites

Symptoms on FRUIT

Problem	Detail	Probable cause
1. Pieces eaten away	Fruit close to ground	Slugs Mice
	Tree fruits	Birds Wasps

Problem	Detail	Probable cause
2. Distorted	With rounded bumps (apples)	Capsid bugs
	Black powder within (sweet corn)	Smut
	Ribbon-like scars (apples)	Sawflies
	Split (tomatoes)	Short of water
3. Discoloured	Uneven ripening (tomatoes)	Virus Nutrient deficiency
4. Mouldy	While on plant (tomatoes)	Grey mould Blight
	While on plant (tree fruits)	Brown rot
	In store	Fungal decay
5. Spotted	Tree fruits Tomato	Scab Ghost spot
6. Maggoty	Tree fruits	Caterpillars (Codling moth)
	Peas	Caterpillars (Pea moth)
	Raspberries	Beetles
7. Dropping prematurely	Pears	Pear midge
	Apples (in early summer)	June drop (normal; not a pest or disease)

Symptoms on FLOWERS

Problem	Detail	Probable cause
1. Drooping	General	Short of water End of flowering period
2. Tattered	Masses of tiny holes	Caterpillars
	Large pieces torn away	Birds
3. Removed entire	Usually discarded nearby	Birds
4. Distorted	Usually only a few plants affected in a bed	Virus
5. Discoloured	Powdery white covering	Powdery mildew
6. Mouldy	Fluffy, grey mould	*Botrytis* grey mould

Symptoms on STEMS

Problem	Detail	Probable cause
1. Eaten through	On young plants	Slugs or snails
	On older plants	Mice or rabbits
	On young trees	Rabbits or deer
2. Infested with insects	Green, grey, black or other colour	Aphids
	White, woolly, on tree bark	Woolly aphids
	Flat, encrusted, like limpets	Scale insects
	Large, six legs, worm-like	Caterpillars
3. Rotten	At base; young plants	Stem and foot rot
	On trees and shrubs	Decay fungus
4. Blister on bark of trees	More or less spherical	Gall
	Target-like	Canker
5. Dying back	General	Short of water
6. Abnormal growth	Like bird's nests	Witches' broom
	Leafy plant	Mistletoe
	Buds swollen (blackcurrants)	Big bud

Symptoms on ROOTS and BULBS

Problem	Detail	Probable cause
1. Decayed	General	Decay fungi
2. Parts eaten away	General	Small soil pests (millepedes, wireworms, leatherjackets)
	Corms and bulbs	Vine weevils
3. With irregular swellings	Brassicas and wallflowers	Clubroot
	Potatoes	Eelworms
	Peas and beans	Root nodules
4. Maggoty	General	Fly larvae
5. With warty spots	Root vegetables	Scab
6. Irregularly distorted	Root vegetables	See page 72

SEEDS AND SEEDLINGS

Seeds are relatively robust structures, clearly designed to survive adverse conditions, although they are quite likely to be eaten whole by larger pests. But as soon as they take in water before germinating, they become more delicate and are then vulnerable to attack by pests and diseases of many kinds. The young seedling itself is, of course, even more vulnerable and the loss of baby plants at this stage probably causes gardeners more sadness and disappointment than anything else. These youngsters must, therefore, be protected in a variety of ways if they are to survive.

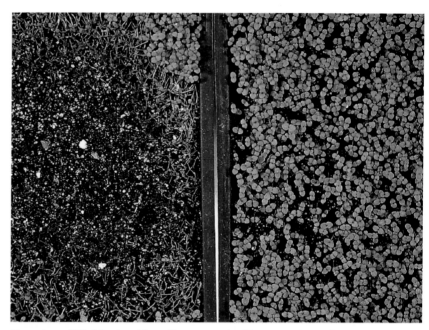

Damping-off (left) arises if seedlings are raised in contaminated compost

Damping-off

AFFECTS
Seedlings of all types.

RECOGNITION
Sometimes seeds become diseased and die before they germinate or, at least, before the seedlings have emerged above the soil. Alternatively, the young seedlings die after they have begun to grow. Sometimes mould growth is visible whereas, in other instances, the stem appears dry and pinched and the seedling shrivels away. Although damping-off is a seedling problem, the rotting of cuttings before they strike is brought about by similar causes.

POSSIBLE CONFUSION WITH
Any pest that removes and eats seeds after they have been sown. If the problem is extensive, it may be worth scraping away the soil to see if the dead seeds can be found.

NON-CHEMICAL TREATMENT
In seed boxes, cleanliness is the key to avoiding damping-off: don't raise seedlings in boxes in garden soil, or re-use seedling compost; always wash seed trays and pots with proprietary garden disinfectant before re-using them; don't allow seed boxes to become very damp through over-watering or leaving covers over them for too long; and don't forget that young seedlings need light – it's important not to leave them covered for too long. If a patch of diseased seedlings occurs in a seed box, dispose of all the seedlings in the box and start again. Much damping-off type of damage to cuttings can be avoided by ensuring that the compost mix used for striking them is very free-draining.

CHEMICAL TREATMENT
Strictly limited. Although most gardeners these days buy bags of proprietary compost, home-made mixtures can be sterilised effectively by placing them in a domestic oven at 150°C (gas regulo 2) for an hour or in a microwave oven at full setting, allowing seven minutes per kilo of compost (which must be in a non-metallic tray). Wash off all old soil and roots from seed boxes and pots; use a proprietary garden disinfectant to remove any lingering infective agents then give the containers a final rinse in clean water before use. Protect cuttings by dipping them in a rooting powder containing fungicide.

RESISTANT VARIETIES
None are resistant, and annual bedding plants and some vegetables such as lettuces, brassicas and peas and

beans are particularly prone. Soft, fleshy cuttings are most likely to suffer from damping-off rots.

Birds, mice and other rodents, cats

AFFECT
Seeds and seedlings of all kinds; they are liable to be damaged, uprooted and/or eaten.

RECOGNITION
The effects are usually self-evident and seed-eating birds such as wood pigeons or sparrows will often be seen in the act of theft. Mice and voles tend to prefer peas and beans and usually work unseen at night; as a result, their activities are often not suspected until the plants fail to emerge and inspection reveals that the seeds have vanished. Cats are more generally destructive for their unearthing of seeds and seedlings

is indiscriminate and incidental to their use of freshly disturbed earth as toilets.

POSSIBLE CONFUSION WITH
Some forms of damping-off that bring about the death of seeds.

NON-CHEMICAL TREATMENT
Protection and prevention are the keys to control, for while small rodents can be killed in traps, I don't advise this because of the risk of injuring birds and domestic animals. Cover seed beds with wire-netting, although a mesh as small as 1cm (¼in) will be needed to exclude mice. Cotton and similar materials may trap and injure birds and shouldn't be used, although bird scaring devices are worth trying if they don't upset your neighbours. Much the best way to deter cats is with one of the modern electronic devices that emit an incredibly high-pitched tone, inaudible to humans but annoying, although harmless, to cats. The equipment

Battery operated cat deterrent emits a sound inaudible to humans

comprises a small plastic box, attached to a peg which is left in place in the soil. Power is supplied either by batteries or, even better, through a lead from a small transformer.

CHEMICAL CONTROL
Fungicide and insecticide seed dressings recommended against damping-off will render seeds unattractive to rodents. I find chemical repellents are of little value and are only worth trying if all else fails.

■ Remember that all birds are legally protected and you mustn't attempt to kill or harm them. And remember, too, that cats are domestic animals and one that is your pest will be someone else's pet. A tactful word to the owner may be much more beneficial than a vindictive campaign against his animal.

Rodents can be caught in humane traps and then released elsewhere

Cutworms, leatherjackets, wireworms, millepedes and woodlice

AFFECT
Seedlings of all types; wireworms and millepedes are also very troublesome in damaging potato tubers. Ornamental bulbs, corms and tubers may also be attacked by some of these pests.

RECOGNITION
Cutworms are moth caterpillars, leatherjackets are the larvae of crane flies (daddy-long-legs) and wireworms are the larvae of click beetles, but the damage that they all cause is similar. Seedlings turn yellow and remain stunted or may wilt and keel over as their roots are damaged or the stems severed at the base. Woodlice will also sever young stems but, more commonly, nibble away at roots, stems and leaves, so causing a general weakening of the plant. Millepedes usually remain in the soil and damage roots or extend wounds caused by other pests.

POSSIBLE CONFUSION WITH
Other forms of root damage, such as that brought about by slugs (see opposite), and some fungal rotting diseases which also cause seedlings to wilt or keel over. Excavation of the soil around the roots usually reveals the creatures responsible: dingy brown cutworm caterpillars and leatherjacket larvae or the rather horny, wriggling, yellowish wireworms. Many types of

Leatherjacket larvae tend to be most serious in hot, dry seasons

small creature will also nibble seeds and seedlings, but millepedes and woodlice are the commonest and will usually be found associated with the symptoms of their activities.

NON-CHEMICAL TREATMENT
You will help limit the activities of all of these pests by regular and thorough cultivation of the soil to ensure that they are brought to the surface and so

Brought to the soil surface, wireworms will be eaten by garden birds

exposed to birds and other predators. Above all, however, garden debris of all kinds must be routinely cleared away, as it provides the pests with places in which they can hide and breed. I often say that a tidy garden is likely to be a healthy one, and this is certainly true with regard to these pests.

CHEMICAL TREATMENT

Although you can buy fungicidal and insecticidal dusts for treating seed, you will generally find that, if the problem is severe and common enough, the seed companies themselves will supply seed already treated. In any event, the effects of such treatments are likely to be confined to the seeds themselves and won't offer much protection to the emerging seedlings. Mixing insecticidal dusts or granules into the soil of seed beds should give longer-lasting protection but this, too, must be combined with cultural measures; and

it isn't something that I like to do with edible crops.

Slugs and snails

The holes that slugs and snails eat into stems and leaves commonly occur in very large numbers, and result in the plants having a generally tattered appearance. The major clue to their activity, and the one that differentiates them from all other pests, is the presence of silvery slime trails. There are several chemical products available for controlling them, but all contain either metaldehyde or methiocarb in pellet, liquid, powder or flake form. The major drawback is that they are potentially harmful to domestic livestock, the pellets especially so, and vegetables and strawberries should not be eaten for at least two weeks after pellets have been used on or adjacent

to them. This, however, is unlikely to be an issue with seedlings.

If you do have to resort to chemical controls, try to use liquid formulations if there is a likelihood of pets or other animals picking up pellets. Alternatively, tuck the pellets close to the plants but beneath a piece of slate or similar material to conceal them.

Such substances as soot and ashes that are powdery and adhere to the slimy bodies of slugs and snails are fairly effective deterrents, as are minutely spiny twigs such as gorse, and these can usefully be placed around vulnerable seedlings. Although a biological slug control is now available (see page 14), this is unlikely to be of value specifically for seedling protection. Straightforward trapping can also be effective. Use upturned grapefruit skins or small dishes filled with beer. Inspect them each morning, remove each night's catch and dispose of them.

Several species of slug find their way into seed boxes to feed on soft, young plants

BEDDING PLANTS

"In development terms, bedding plants are one step further on from seedlings, but they never build up the more or less permanent rootstock, bulb, corm or tuber that characterises herbaceous perennials. They include all the familiar annual, half-hardy bedding plants, the vigorously growing, hardy annual summer flowers such as sweet peas, biennials such as wallflowers and sweet Williams and those plants such as pelargoniums that, although strictly tender perennials, are more usually grown as annuals in this country. They have one important common feature in their facility for rapid growth, but this attribute can bring its own problems, for the resulting tissues are intrinsically soft and prone to pest and disease attack. One important way in which you can minimise this risk is to ensure that the plants are well hardened-off: accustom them gradually to outdoor temperatures in a cold frame before planting them out. A well-toughened bedding plant is, I think, well on the way to having a healthy life."

Wallflowers suffer from problems as they are in the ground for so long

(page 32). The most important biennial garden flowers are wallflowers, which can be affected by clubroot (page 74) and by a problem known as winter killing, the death of plants during cold weather, generally thought to be caused by *Botrytis* grey mould (page 59). The major remaining problems of bedding plants are all related, in one way another, to the early stages of growth and establish-ment and it is these that I have considered here.

Scope

Many of the problems that affect bedding plants are described in detail elsewhere in the book; these include soil pests such as cutworms, leather-jackets and wireworms (page 28), slugs and snails (page 29), mice, voles and birds (sparrows are notorious for nipping off flower buds, page 27), small, leaf-eating caterpillars (page 68), aphids (page 33), and powdery mildew

Petal spotting by Botrytis *is disfiguring and leads to decay later*

Root, stem and foot rots

AFFECT
Almost every type of bedding plant if the conditions are sufficiently moist but the most serious losses probably arise with sweet peas and other hardy annuals when sown in the autumn.

RECOGNITION
The name is descriptive, for a black rotting affects the roots, stems and/or the stem base, which is often called the 'foot', and may spread from there to cause the leaves and flowers to decay, the complete plant ultimately being lost as a consequence. Sometimes individual plants may be affected; or an entire bed of plants might fade away.

POSSIBLE CONFUSION WITH
Although other problems may cause the loss of a few plants, the blackening of the roots is diagnostic.

NON-CHEMICAL TREATMENT
Because the causes of these problems are many and varied, there is no overall means either of avoidance or control. Nonetheless, it's sensible to take certain general precautions. Even when plants have been carefully and correctly hardened off, as I mentioned earlier, they shouldn't be given too great a transplanting shock as they will then be vulnerable to the soil fungi that are responsible for the rotting, and to the pests whose initial activity may allow the fungi access to the inner tissues. One way that you can avoid this transplanting shock is by not planting into too cold or too wet a soil. Even at

Waterlogged compost can result in root rot and feeble transplants

the end of spring and the beginning of summer, when many of the plants will be transplanted, spells of cold weather are still common. It's much better to wait an extra week rather than suffer serious loss. Also, try to ensure that your plants aren't under stress at the time of planting: make sure that they have been pricked out early into sufficiently large trays or pots and also that they are in an appropriate seedling compost.

CHEMICAL TREATMENT
No chemicals available to gardeners will have any effect on the problem.

Pansy sickness and Aster wilt

Pansy sickness is a very common problem that affects pansies and sometimes other forms of *Viola*, which fail to establish properly after being transplanted into a bed that has previously contained pansies. Aster wilt is an almost identical problem that affects bedding asters (that is, those varieties such as 'Duchess' that are derived from *Callistephus chinensis*. It doesn't affect the true asters or Michaelmas daisies). Both problems are probably similar in origin to rose sickness and the replant problems that sometimes occur when old fruit orchards are re-stocked. Although some modern aster varieties have high levels of wilt resistance, there are no comparable resistant pansies but both problems can generally be circumvented by raising the plants in individual pots and planting them out in the entire block of compost which gives them a disease-free base from which they can become established. Within limits, the larger the pot, the larger the base that the plant has from which to grow but in practice, you will find that a 10cm diameter pot is about right.

HERBACEOUS PERENNIALS

" *Herbaceous perennials have been one of the great glories of the summer garden for centuries, although never more so since their virtues were championed by the likes of Gertrude Jekyll and William Robinson in the latter years of the nineteenth and early years of the twentieth century. Today, they tend to share the mixed border with shrubs rather than have an area dedicated entirely to themselves. They remain extremely valuable plants yet they have always been prone to certain pest and disease problems. Like annuals, their rapid growth and soft tissues make them particularly vulnerable to attack, but their saving grace is that they die down at the end of the season, to be renewed afresh in the following. Most of the problems to which herbaceous perennials are subject are, nonetheless, common to many other types of garden plant and are described in detail in other sections of the book so I simply provide notes on them here. The special problems associated with bulbous perennials are described on page 34.* "

Slugs and snails

Although these aren't usually serious pests on established plants, there are a few significant exceptions. Hostas have a magnetic attraction for both slugs and snails and although some varieties are claimed to be resistant, it is all a matter of degree and I believe that no hosta can be guaranteed immune from attack. Much the best way to circumvent the problem and, incidentally, grow the plants very attractively, is in containers, raised on small 'feet'. The young shoots of other herbaceous perennials are also vulnerable to attack and some protection (page 29) will be needed when delphiniums, dahlias and chrysanthemums are just emerging.

Leaf spots

Spotting may occur on the leaves of most garden plants, but only hellebores among herbaceous perennials are likely to need treatment, in the form of a spray with a copper-containing fungicide. The very common spotting on the leaves of hollyhocks is a symptom of hollyhock rust (see opposite).

Earwigs

Although they aren't serious garden pests, the familiar shiny brown earwigs are very fond of making a home on and in dahlia and chrysanthemum flowers, where they may nibble the petals and can cause alarm if flowers are brought into the house. Contact insecticides will control them but should be used in moderation, for they can be disfiguring to the blooms. Much the best plan is trapping: use upturned plastic plant pots, stuffed with hay, straw or shredded paper and placed on canes among the plants. The earwigs will hide in the pots during daytime, when they can be removed and destroyed.

Mildew

Powdery, white mildew growth is very common on many herbaceous perennials although very commonly, as on doronicums, it occurs chiefly after flowering and so causes little harm. Phlox and Michaelmas daisies can be affected very severely but resistant varieties are available, especially among

Earwigs hide during the daytime and must be trapped at night

Lupin mildew is unavoidable but is usually too late to affect flowering

Michaelmas daisies: choose forms of *Aster* x *frikartii* or the dwarf *Aster thomsonii* 'Nanus'. For moderate attacks on other plants, spray with fungicide containing carbendazim.

Aphids

Aphids will be familiar every summer and many different species occur in the herbaceous border, with individual species often restricted to particular types of plants. In recent years, an introduced North American species, the truly enormous lupin aphid has become a serious and dramatic pest. Early and late season perennials, such as aquilegias and dahlias, are often severely affected on the succulent young shoots. Spray with contact insecticide as soon as the first infestations are seen.

Rust

Rust diseases aren't commonly serious on herbaceous perennials, although there are two exceptions: the rusts of hollyhocks (and related plants such as mallows and sidalceas), and antirr-hinums, which can be devastating in some seasons. The first causes small orange dimples and the latter powdery, brown pustules on the leaves, which soon wither and drop. It is important to look out for the first signs of the disease and spray hollyhocks promptly with the fungicide penconazole. Antirr-hinum rust can be avoided by selecting modern varieties bred with resistance.

Virus

Dahlias, chrysanthemums and carnations, like all vegetatively propagated plants, are subject to virus diseases which give rise to problems such as distorted leaves and flowers and poor growth. These are only likely to be seen on old plants or if gardeners have inadvertently taken cuttings from diseased plants; most reputable suppliers will sell only healthy stock. Any plants suspected of having virus contamination should be destroyed immediately before the disease is spread to healthy individuals.

Soil pests

Like slugs and snails, other soil-inhabiting pests belonging to other groups such as wireworms, cutworms, vine weevils and leatherjackets can be troublesome, especially to young plants. They can, however, be kept within bounds by the application of soil insecticide dust to the soil or sometimes by use of the biological control for vine weevils (page 14).

Hollyhock rust can be checked by responding at the first signs of attack

BULBS, CORMS AND TUBERS

" "There are few sights in gardening more cheering than the emergence of the first bulbs in spring. I always think it's because they follow a period of such un-ashamed climatic misery that they are better appreciated than their counterparts in the autumn. But there are also few sights more depressing than the emergence of leaves alone; sometimes of de-pressing sickly hue. Established flowering bulbs can be affected by some of the same types of problems as herbaceous perennials and other garden plants, so I have concen-trated here on the pests and diseases that attack the bulbous body itself, and provided notes on the remainder. I should add that although I shall call them all 'bulbs' I include also the structures that strictly may be corms or tubers. " "

Bulbs and corms showing signs of disease lesions should not be planted

Bulb rot

Being so soft and fleshy, bulbs are prone to fungal and bacterial rotting, both in store and when planted in the garden. Storage decay can generally be avoided by inspecting the bulbs carefully before they are stored, handling them with care, and rejecting any that are damaged. Sound, well-dried bulbs stored in bags or on trays should then be safe from all pests and diseases except rodents (voles adore crocuses), but those that are stored in peat, ashes or other material should be dusted both with sulphur as a fungicide and an insecticide dust before being laid down. My notes on fruit and vegetable storage will also be helpful (page 82),

but one significant difference from fruit and vegetables is that bulbs may safely be treated with pesticide dusts.

Decay arising after planting can be minimised by ensuring that bulbs that require free-draining soils aren't planted in wet ones and that all bulbs have a small handful of sand placed beneath them at planting time. Fritillaries and other bulbs with a depression at the stem base are best planted on their sides to prevent water from accumulating there and causing rot. Control of pests such as narcissus fly (see opposite) will also help to lessen the damage that is so often the prelude to decay.

Bulb pests

Although millepedes, woodlice and other soil-inhabiting creatures will contentedly attack bulbs and cause some damage, generally this only occurs when they have been planted in less than ideal conditions and the plants may already be stressed. However, this type of damage only becomes serious when it allows decay fungi to infect the bulbs and lead to significant decay (see left). Much the most important bulb attacking pests, in all circumstances, are the narcissus fly and the vine weevil.

Narcissus flies

These look rather like tiny bumble bees and they emerge in early summer, the females landing near to narcissi, hyacinths and sometimes other bulbs too, in order to lay their eggs. The larvae soon hatch and tunnel down to attack the bulb, usually through the hole left where the old flower stalk has rotted away. The damage they cause to the embryo flower bud within is one of the commonest explanations for 'blindness': the appearance of foliage (which may itself be distorted) but no flowers. Although difficult to control totally, narcissus flies can be discouraged very effectively by the simple expedient of raking soil around the plants as the flowers and foliage begin to fade in order to block the entry tunnels.

Vine weevils

In recent years these have become among the most troublesome of all pests and their larvae can cause serious damage to some bulbous plants, especially cyclamen. Although dusting with soil insecticide around the plants and around the tubers when planting may have some effect, much the better option is to use one of the nematode-based biological control systems now available (page 14).

Virus

As with other plants that are propagated vegetatively, virus contamination may build up in stocks of bulbous plants over a period of years. It's most important to check them each season after they emerge therefore and remove any individuals showing distorted, yellowed, crumpled or otherwise unusual flowers or leaves.

Among other symptoms that may be seen on bulbous plants and that are described in detail elsewhere are rust (page 83), leaf attacking beetles (on lilies especially) (page 83), and grey mould or similar diseases (tulips are often attacked) (page 59).

Both fungal attack and virus can result in tulips with distorted shoots. They should be dug up and destroyed

ROSES

"Although roses have declined slightly in popularity in recent years, no plant remains so close to a gardener's heart and there have never been so many good varieties available. Largely because they have been subjected to such intense breeding in the pursuit of improved flower quality, over the years roses have become prone to considerable pest and disease problems. Fortunately, modern variety evaluation attaches great importance to resistance and it's unlikely that a new variety could 'escape' on to the market today if it were significantly problem prone. Nonetheless, many of the most beautiful roses aren't modern and there are varieties still grown that have been propagated vegetatively since the thirteenth century. Small wonder that pest and disease difficulties remain."

Rose diseases

Although roses are liable to be affected by some of the common diseases that attack other types of shrub, such as shoot dieback, stem and root rot, silver leaf and cankers, they infrequently cause much damage. There are three other, readily identifiable diseases that account for almost all of the concern in gardens: mildew, black spot and rust. To many gardeners these three, quite different problems are inseparable, although rust is recognised as the least common. None of them is likely to infect other types of plant although related forms of mildew, rust and leaf spot can occur on other species.

Mildew

RECOGNITION

It's unlikely that any gardener needs to be told how to recognise this disease, probably the commonest of all garden problems. It's rarely seen before mid-spring in most parts of the country, and climbers or other roses grown in dry, sheltered spots, such as close to walls, are almost always the earliest to show the symptoms and are, overall, particularly prone to attack. The powdery, white mildew growth is most obvious on the leaves, which tend to curl and take on a purple tint, but the infection can also spread to the stems, buds and flowers.

Rose mildew is ubiquitous and affects all parts of the plant

NON-CHEMICAL TREATMENT

Try to avoid highly nitrogenous fertilizers such as dried blood or ammonium sulphate; balanced proprietary rose fertilizers are much more reliable and don't encourage soft, susceptible growth. On dry sites, always endeavour to improve the soil moisture retentiveness with mulches and ensure that climbing roses are attached to trellis raised from the wall surface on battens to facilitate a free flow of air around the plants.

CHEMICAL TREATMENT

See opposite.

RESISTANT VARIETIES

Resistance to mildew is scattered among most of the major rose groups. Rather than pick out odd varieties from the many available, I refer you to Book 7 of this series *Best Roses*. See also page 38.

Black spot

RECOGNITION

Black spots on rose leaves first appear towards late spring in most parts of the country and, if allowed to develop unchecked, they gradually spread to affect a large part of the leaf which turns characteristically yellow and may eventually drop. The flowering and overall vigour of the plant soon begins to suffer as a result.

NON-CHEMICAL TREATMENT

Because the black spot fungus survives during the winter on the shoots rather than the leaves, hard pruning in spring will help considerably in limiting its

Spray early against black spot and prevent the spores from spreading

impact. Therefore, much to many gardeners' surprise, the collection and destruction of fallen leaves will not, in itself, make much difference.

CHEMICAL TREATMENT
See right.

RESISTANT VARIETIES
As with mildew (see opposite), resistance to black spot occurs in varieties belonging to most groups. Detailed information on disease resistance is given in Book 7 of the series, *Best Roses*, although it's certainly true that overall, yellow-flowered varieties are most prone to black spot and the majority of modern varieties have much more disease resistance than old ones. See also page 38.

Rust

RECOGNITION
The first signs of rose rust in the spring are small, bright orange pustules on the young leaves and shoots but these are usually overlooked and most gardeners will be familiar only with the yellow and black, pin-head-sized powdery pustules that develop beneath the leaves later. The leaves drop more rapidly as a result of rust infection than they seem to do with the other rose diseases.

NON-CHEMICAL TREATMENT
Any diseased leaves should be collected up and burned for, unlike black spot, the rust disease fungus does survive through the winter on fallen foliage. As with mildew, the over-application of nitrogen-rich fertilizers can predispose plants to rust infection.

RESISTANT VARIETIES
See page 38.

Chemical treatment of rose diseases

It's important to consider the three main rose diseases as a group, because not many gardeners will want to buy a product that isn't effective against them all or, at least, against the two that occur most frequently, mildew and black spot. The chemicals available vary in their effectiveness against the three problems: overall, the best against mildew and black spot is probably carbendazim, followed closely by bupirimate, triforine and sulphur.

Rust is harder to control and the two most effective treatments that I have used are penconazole and myclobutanil. Do bear in mind that aphids (page 38) will almost certainly be a problem too and a good proprietary product that combines a fungicide with an insecticide as an overall rose treatment makes sound sense. There are several very good products on the market.

Rust is usually the least serious of the three main diseases

Resistance to diseases

The subject of disease resistance is probably more relevant to roses than to any other group of garden plants. This is partly because the three diseases of mildew, black spot and rust are extremely widespread and damaging, partly because resistance to them does exist in the rose genus, and is therefore available to plant breeders, and partly because no other group of plants (certainly not of ornamentals) is subject to such rigorous assessment in trials of new varieties. Having said this, it would take many pages to itemise the huge number of varieties now available and indicate their relative resistance to black spot, mildew and rust. I shall, therefore, simply offer guidelines and assume that serious rose growers will belong to one or other of the important societies, the Royal National Rose Society and the Royal Horticultural Society, from which detailed trials data can be obtained.

If you select only the latest rose varieties, you will be unlikely to experience serious disease problems, as no new roses that score badly in disease assessments are likely to be released. Nonetheless, resistance isn't static and over a period of years, even highly resistant varieties can succumb, especially to mildew, as new strains of the disease fungus arise. A classic example of this is the orange Hybrid Tea 'Super Star'. This was introduced in 1960 to wide acclaim and won the Royal National Rose Society President's International Trophy for the best new seedling rose of the year and a gold

medal. It was awarded an astonishing 18 points out of 20 for freedom from disease. A mere 10 years later, in the Society's *Selected List of Varieties*, it was suggested that it 'may need protection from mildew'. Today, you will be lucky to find a plant not severely affected. This, therefore, is the price you may have to pay if you choose, for sentimental or other reasons, to select the older among modern rose varieties.

With the truly old roses, the shrub varieties that, in some instances, date back many centuries, you will have to take pot luck. There are susceptible and resistant varieties in all groups, although the shrubs derived from the Japanese *Rosa rugosa* (which admittedly are more modern mainly twentieth century types) are generally highly resistant to disease (and, unusually, to aphids also). Do read catalogue descriptions particularly carefully and refer to Book 7 in this series, *Best Roses,* where I have given more specific information for a wide range of varieties. The only generalisation I will make here is that yellow roses tend to be more prone to black spot than those of any other colour.

Rose aphids

Although a great many different types of insect will attack roses from time to time, there is no doubt that aphids hugely outnumber all others. It's small wonder that they cause such problems because at least seven different aphid species find roses to their liking and you will very often see green, black and pinkish aphids together on the same shoots.

RECOGNITION

As with mildew, I certainly won't have to describe aphids to anyone who has ever gardened, although it's perhaps worth adding that they can survive on the plants all year round in favourable conditions. Just as with mildew, it's on climbing roses or others in sheltered positions that problems are most likely to occur.

As the insects accumulate on the succulent young shoots, the growth inevitably becomes weakened and distorted and, although plants won't be killed by even severe infestations of aphids, they can soon begin to look a very sorry mess. Interestingly, and fortunately, rose aphids don't seem to carry virus diseases as much as some other aphid species. They multiply with extraordinary speed, however, until early summer.

Leaf cutter bees can be tolerated although the damage is unsightly

Slugworm sawfly larvae erode the leaf surface but are seldom serious

NON-CHEMICAL TREATMENT

Keeping plants open-structured by pruning will always help to minimise aphid attack, as will attaching climbers in such a way as to allow free air flow around them, but this will never be a complete answer. Hosing plants down regularly will clear away the bulk of the aphids in a colony and, if it is done repeatedly in the late spring and early summer, you may be able to keep overall aphid populations in check for the rest of the summer.

CHEMICAL TREATMENT

Almost any contact insecticide will be reasonably effective against aphids so you have the option of choosing between synthetic chemicals and natural products, such as derris or those based on natural soaps. Among synthetic chemicals, however, is a particularly valuable one, pirimicarb, which has the virtue of almost complete selectivity, killing aphids but leaving other insects unharmed. Do bear in mind that rose diseases will almost certainly need controlling too and it makes sense to choose a product that combines your chosen insecticide with a fungicide.

RESISTANT VARIETIES

Resistance to aphid attack is much more elusive and much less well recorded than resistance to rose diseases. Of the main groups of roses, the Rugosas are seldom attacked by aphids, and there are clearly differences among some other groups, even if these aren't well documented. I find the short climbing rose 'Aloha', for instance, the most resistant among modern roses that I have grown.

Other rose pests

Rose leaf-hoppers These pests cause a fine white mottling on the leaf surfaces but routine sprays for aphid control should provide a satisfactory check against them.

Leaf-cutter bees take small, semi-circular pieces from the edges of the leaves but, although disfiguring, little damage is caused and no treatment is in fact necessary.

Leaf-rolling sawflies cause unmistakable and characteristic distortion in which the leaflets roll inwards, cigar-fashion; and this occurs wherever the female insect has probed, irrespective of whether any eggs have been laid. Unfortunately, control is impossible but severely damaged leaves usually drop and little damage to the plant seems to occur.

The green larvae of **rose slug sawflies** will sometimes be seen browsing on the leaf surface; while **capsid bugs** cause leaf tattering but both appear too erratically to justify control measures. Many other insect pests may be seen occasionally on roses, but treatment is rarely needed.

'Aloha' has disease and pest resistance and is a fine modern rose

LAWNS

"Lawns are unique among garden plants. Indeed, so different are they that many gardeners scarcely think of them as plants, but as objects. This is largely because of the way we treat them, but there are horticultural reasons for their uniqueness too. Grasses are closely related to cereals and many of the pest and disease problems that affect them are similar to those that affect cereal crops. Unlike cereals, however, the tops are continually being mown off, so the various foliage problems, like rust and mildew, that are so devastating in cereal crops, rarely cause significant damage on lawns. It tends to be problems arising at and just below soil level that are most important but because it's impossible to separate the individual plants within a lawn, the pests and diseases are essentially those that affect the entire turf."

Dead patches of turf

One dead patch of turf looks pretty much like another, and a measure of common sense is needed to determine the cause. Yellow patches that arise during dry weather are probably the result of leatherjacket activity (page 28) and excavating a small area should reveal the insects. The best treatment is to water the patch thoroughly in the evening, cover it with a plastic sheet and collect up the larvae which come to the surface during the night. They are then most usefully put in a dish on the bird table. If leatherjackets don't seem to be the cause, ensure that some

chemical has not been spilt on the area (see my comments on page 19) but if this too seems improbable, a fungal disease may be the answer. There are several of these, some occurring during wet weather in the spring, others in dry weather during the summer and some accompanied by pink or grey fungal growth. Apply a spray strength mixture of carbendazim after mowing and, as a routine preventative against fungal attack, don't apply nitrogenous fertilizer after early autumn as this will encourage susceptible soft growth.

Establishment problems

These are the difficulties that arise when a new lawn is sown (newly laid turf is likely to suffer from a shortage of water, not pests and diseases) and they are considered on page 28 together with the general problems associated with seeds and seedlings. These problems underline the fact that it is trickier and less reliable to establish lawns from seed rather than turf.

Fairy rings are disfiguring but it's impossible to eradicate them

Red thread disease is rather common in newly laid turf

Fairy rings

More-or-less circular rings of toadstools and darker grass can occur on any type of short, cropped or mown grass. Many people welcome them, others don't mind, but some feel that the appearance is disfiguring and should be removed. Feel free, if you must, to brush away the toadstools but you won't eradicate the fungal growth from the soil. Complete removal of fairy rings is very, very difficult. The procedure is long and laborious, involves chemicals that aren't available to gardeners and is only partly effective. It is better to spike thoroughly in the area of dead grass and apply additional lawn fertilizer in this region. In passing, I should add that whilst most fairy rings are caused by an edible species of toadstool, *Marasmius oreades*, not all are and it is easy to collect poisonous species along with the *Marasmius* unless you have expert guidance.

Lichen and algae

Although strictly neither pest nor disease, lichen or, less commonly, the green slime of algae can be a cause of concern. Their control is usually effected by one of the proprietary moss killers based on dichlorophen but the presence of the growths, like that of moss, should be taken as an indication that the lawn is in need of feeding, draining, possibly less close mowing, less shade and/or some aeration.

Moles

One of the most emotive of garden problems, moles cause the most damage in lawns although they can be troublesome almost anywhere in the garden and have even been found under greenhouses. I shan't for one moment pretend that I have a consistently reliable answer but among the measures that have worked for at least some gardeners are:

■ Trapping, with calliper traps, although some expertise is needed to locate the best runs in which to place the trap and, in rural areas, a farm worker or someone similar who is practised in the matter may well help. But trapping is of no use, of course, if you are averse to killing the creatures.

■ Foul-smelling deterrents, among which you can take your pick, from old fish heads to moth repellents and proprietary smoke cartridges. I'm told that pain-relieving ointments are very effective.

■ An electronic deterrent, a rather expensive device which is inserted into the runs and emits an ultrasonic pulse, will sometimes drive moles away; although they may still return.

■ A cat; far and away the best answer in my experience, provided you can obtain a cat that is a natural 'moler'; some are, some aren't.

Electronic mole deterrent

TREES AND SHRUBS

"Poor is the garden that lacks at least one tree; and impossible is the garden that lacks some shrubs. Yet the relative longevity and permanent woody structure of trees and shrubs mean that they are constantly at the mercy of pests and diseases. Some of these problems are shared with fruit trees but, as the group includes conifers and other evergreen species in addition to deciduous types, a further, distinct group of pests and diseases may occur. The fact that many types are regularly pruned affords opportunity for diseases to enter. Damage doesn't usually arise rapidly and, if detected early, extensive harm may be prevented. The most serious of all tree and shrub problems, honey fungus and Phytophthora root death are, however, difficult to control."

Wound paints are unnecessary and may even cause harm to the tree

Rots, decay, and wound treatment

Apart from the special case of honey fungus, many other wood-rotting fungi can cause damage to garden trees, but on the trunk and branches rather than the roots and so, in many cases, it's perfectly possible to save them. Any branch bearing large fungal growths is likely to be extensively decayed and should be removed. If the decay is seen to extend into the trunk, it may be possible to gouge out the affected tissue, if it is clearly well entrenched, the tree is better felled because it will be inherently unstable and likely to be blown down in a gale. If the tree is large or in a rather confined position, do obtain professional assistance; major

tree surgery definitely isn't a task for the amateur.

When branches are removed, they should never be sawn flush with the trunk, as this removes the natural wound-healing tissues. The branch should be removed as close as possible to the 'collar', the small raised swelling at the branch base. As it's now generally accepted that wound-sealing 'paints' are of little value and may indeed be harmful, leave the wound open to heal naturally.

Honey fungus

AFFECTS
Almost every species of woody plant, and damage can also occur occasionally

on herbaceous perennials. Honey fungus ranks among the top three garden diseases in seriousness.

RECOGNITION
Most commonly, the first indication of the possible presence of honey fungus in a garden is a dead or nearly dead tree or shrub. Then comes the real detective work. If the toadstools are present at or close to the base of the plant, the matter is relatively straight-forward; provided the toadstools can be identified accurately. They are usually up to 15cm (6in) high with a cap up to 15cm (6in) in diameter; tawny or yellowish in colour with darker scales or specks towards the centre. Beneath the cap, the gills are white or yellowish and the stem usually bears a large, whitish, yellow-bordered ring. If the bark is peeled away at the base of the affected plant, whitish fungal growth or, more characteristically, flat, narrow, ribbon-like structures may be seen, while in the surrounding soil, objects similar to black bootlaces may occur. The fungus is less likely to attack old trees than young ones but is most unlikely to attack any trees or shrubs within a couple of years after planting.

POSSIBLE CONFUSION WITH
A great many things. All manner of toadstools commonly grow at the bases of both live and dead trees. Most are quite harmless; some are positively beneficial to the plants. A good guide book to mushrooms and toadstools will help here. Decay in the trunks of trees more than about 60cm (24in) above ground level is unlikely to be caused by honey fungus and the total absence of toadstools, boot-lace

Bracket-like fungi usually indicate serious decay with the tree

Characteristic strands of honey fungus growth beneath the old bark

strands and fungal growth suggests another cause (see *Phytophthora* root death on page 45 as a likely alternative).

NON-CHEMICAL TREATMENT

Sanitation is the more appropriate term here, for prevention of honey fungus spread rather than cure is the aim. As the disease requires old stumps of broadleaved trees for its initial establishment, every effort should be made to remove the stump when a tree is felled. Once a diseased plant is found, you should attempt as complete as possible a removal of it and its root system. Sometimes, further spread of the problem can be prevented by burying thick plastic sheeting vertically in the soil to a depth of at least 60cm (24in) around the site of an affected tree or shrub; the same procedure may be useful if the source of the problem is in a neighbouring garden. New plants shouldn't be planted on the affected area for at least one, and preferably two or three seasons, to allow the fungus to die away.

CHEMICAL TREATMENT

No 'conventional' fungicides have any effect on honey fungus and opinions vary over the effectiveness of proprietary phenolic emulsions. They are certainly worth trying as soil drenches to limit disease spread to other plants, but do not expect them to cure plants that are already diseased.

RESISTANT VARIETIES

Some trees and shrubs are fairly resistant. These include beech, box, many types of clematis, elaeagnus, hawthorn, holly, ivy, larch, laurel, mahonia, sumac and yew.

Leaf spots

Almost every type of deciduous tree and shrub is likely to develop spotting on the leaves from one cause or another, but relatively few leaf-spotting diseases will cause significant damage to well-established plants. Even those most dramatic in appearance, such as tar spot on maples, seem to have little effect. Only where a tree or shrub is really conspicuously disfigured should any chemical treatment be called for. Even here, recommendations are difficult to make because of the wide variety of possible causes, but two sprays with carbendazim at three week intervals, should be at least moderately effective, if tricky to apply to large trees. Probably the only significant exception to this is the anthracnose disease of weeping willows, where tiny reddish leaf spots accompany the development of grey twig lesions and dying back of the shoots: overall, an excellent set of reasons for not planting weeping willows in gardens. The only chemical spray likely to have any impact on this problem is one containing copper. If the problem is serious, switch to a different type of tree.

Tar spot disfigures maple leaves but causes almost no harm to the tree

Fireblight

AFFECTS
Many trees of the rose family, especially pears, hawthorns, pyracantha, cotoneaster, amelanchier, apples and chaenomeles.

RECOGNITION
Dramatically and suddenly, the plant has the appearance of having been scorched by a flame. Dead blossoms hang from the branches and in warm and moist conditions, drops of glistening slime cover the shrivelled flowers and leaves. Twigs, then branches and, finally, entire trees may die within a very short time.

POSSIBLE CONFUSION WITH
Some types of insect attack and also real fire damage; quite often, especially on hawthorn, reports of fireblight prove to be the result of someone inadvertently setting fire to a hedge with a bonfire. On fruit trees, bacterial blossom wilt is rather similar (see page 55), but in recent years, there has been widespread death of ornamental cherries, especially the variety 'Kanzan'. The symptoms are superficially very like those of fireblight but this disease doesn't affect cherries, and the true cause is unknown although it is probably also bacterial in origin.

TREATMENT
Usually, none possible. Affected branches should be cut out and if this fails to arrest the development of the problem, the tree must be felled. In most areas, it is no longer necessary to notify the authorities of its occurrence.

Waterlogged compost means decay as the roots are unable to breathe

Phytophthora root death

AFFECTS
Almost all species of woody plant. This disease is the most serious tree killer in many parts of the country although most gardeners will never have heard of it by name. The eponymous *Phytophthora* is a microscopic species of soil-inhabiting fungus, related to that causing potato blight.

RECOGNITION
Yellowing and dying back of the foliage of ornamental trees and shrubs, especially conifers, rhododendrons and ornamental cherries. If the roots close to the stem base are exposed, the older portions will appear blackened while some of the young, fibrous rootlets are still white and living. The disease is most likely to be troublesome on wet, poorly drained soils although it can occur on other soil types too.

POSSIBLE CONFUSION WITH
Many other types of die-back. As with honey fungus, identification is not easy, but if all alternative, non-pathological causes can be eliminated, one form or another of *Phytophthora* root death is the most likely explanation.

NON-CHEMICAL TREATMENT
The best answer to root death is avoidance, which is best achieved by buying plants only from reputable nurseries or, if in any doubt, of buying only container-raised plants, which are much less likely to be affected. Thereafter, careful husbandry is essential because once it's established in garden soil, little can be done; there are no chemical treatments. Always slope the soil away from newly planted trees and shrubs because any hollow that forms at the stem base will become waterlogged and create exactly the conditions that the fungus requires. In heavy soils, organic matter should be worked in uniformly over an area much larger than the specific hole itself; so as not to create a sump. And always take care not to water, manure or mulch excessively.

CHEMICAL TREATMENT
No chemical treatment possible.

RESISTANT VARIETIES
Although no woody plants are truly resistant to root death, it is among cypresses that most damage occurs. Ironically, the least affected is the Leyland cypress which could be used to replace other types if all else fails.

Mildew

Although mildew is seen on trees and shrubs much less frequently than it is on herbaceous plants, it can be serious on a few species. Young oaks, sycamores, lilacs, laburnums and Japanese spindle are among those on which it is seen most frequently. As with all tree problems, spraying is impracticable if the plant is very large, but small specimens can be treated with carbendazim or other fungicide.

Mildew can be a problem on young trees in dry summers

Coral spot

AFFECTS
Most woody plants, although relatively uncommon on conifers. In terms of damaging effects, coral spot is one of the most underestimated of diseases.

RECOGNITION
Distinctive, pin-head sized pink pimples cover the bark of affected twigs and branches, which die back as a result. The same symptoms will commonly be seen on dead twigs and branches of all kinds; bundles of pea sticks are very commonly affected.

POSSIBLE CONFUSION WITH
Small, coloured pustules on old, rotten wood in gardens (fence posts and stakes for example); usually yellow but occasionally white or pink. These are caused by harmless fungi, quite unrelated to coral spot, which doesn't affect sawn timber.

NON-CHEMICAL TREATMENT
Always ensure that piles of prunings or other branches or twigs are cleared away promptly. As the fungus must first establish itself on dead twigs and branches before spreading into living tissues, give careful attention to routine pruning, and always cut away old branch stubs. If the symptoms are seen on a growing plant, the affected parts must be removed promptly and burned.

CHEMICAL TREATMENT
Although a preventive treatment for coral spot is neither feasible nor desirable, an affected plant should be sprayed thoroughly with carbendazim once the damaged tissues have been removed, and the spray repeated once more in two or three weeks time.

RESISTANT VARIETIES
No trees can be described as resistant: acers and *Cercis* are especially prone.

Mistletoes and unusual growths

Sometimes, trees will be seen bearing large twiggy or leafy growths that appear 'out of keeping' with the remainder of the plant. They are most likely to be noticed in winter when deciduous trees are leafless, and take two main forms.

The first is mistletoe, a familiar, evergreen, semi-parasitic flowering plant that buries a root-like, feeding organ into the trees. Many people welcome mistletoe on an old apple tree, and its impact on the overall vigour of the plant is likely to be slight.

The second produces growths that look rather like large birds' nests. They are especially common on silver birches and are called witches' brooms. They

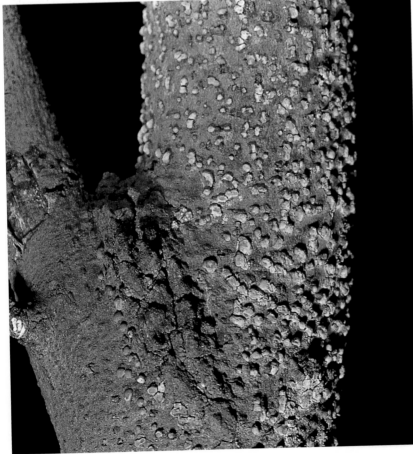

Coral spot attacks dead branches but then spreads into healthy shoots

Large galls only look serious; their effect on the tree is minimal

result from some malfunction of the tree's growth-regulation processes and, like mistletoe, they can be tolerated on garden trees. Indeed, from shoots of some types of witches' broom (especially on conifers), dwarf varieties have been propagated.

Mysterious swellings

Trees and shrubs sometimes become infected with organisms that bring about symptoms that develop slowly and imperceptibly over a considerable period of time. Cankers fall into this category and can be extremely damaging if allowed to develop unchecked. They are described and discussed in the section on tree fruit problems (see page 52). Quite commonly, however, more or less rounded, woody swellings cause concern when first seen but these rarely bring about any real or lasting damage. They are believed to be caused by a particular type of bacterium and are sometimes referred to as 'crown gall'. Attempts to cut them out are not advised as this will usually cause more disfigurement than they cure and they are best left alone.

Caterpillars

Some trees are much more prone than others to the attentions of leaf-eating caterpillars. Not surprisingly, those with large, soft leaves seem most likely to be devoured. It's never worthwhile undertaking routine, protective spraying against caterpillars on garden trees or shrubs, but if you spot signs of serious infestation and damage, one or two sprays with an insecticide such as permethrin or a biological bacterial spray should sufficiently take care of the infestation.

Mammals

Pests that can actually be seen in the act of causing damage are frustrating enough to the gardener, but when damage arises mysteriously during the night, the anguish is compounded. This happens most frequently with trees and shrubs in gardens that are close to fields or natural woodland. The shoot tips may be bruised or the bark stripped from stems and branches. Such damage can be caused by rabbits, grey squirrels or deer, and the only certain means of protection is by their total exclusion. To exclude deer, fences need to be at least 1.8m (6ft) high, whereas rabbit netting should be made of small mesh and be buried to a depth of about 30cm (12in). Squirrels, of course, will pay no heed to such futile barriers and netting must be draped over plants to keep them away. Trees or shrubs with an appreciable length of straight stem may, however, be protected from bark stripping with spiral tree protectors.

Deer cause much harm by chewing away the bark from low branches

"All of the fruit trees grown in British gardens belong to the rose family and so, as you might expect, they share some common problems. Apples are very close relatives of pears and have more problems in common with them than they do with plums, cherries, damsons, and the other stone fruits. Orchard trees are affected by such conditions as cankers which, in one form or another, are common to ornamental and forest trees, but none are closely related to soft fruits, which tend to suffer from a different range of problems. Most of the common problems that arise when fruit is stored (see page 82) originate when it is still growing on the tree, so care and attention at this stage will reap benefits later. Fruit trees, with their long life and soft, fleshy produce are particularly prone to many pest and disease problems and so it will come as no surprise that this is the largest section of the book."

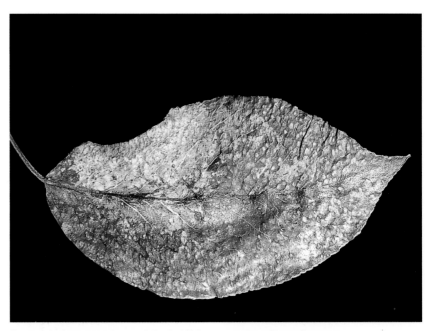

Severe and repeated attack by leaf blister mite weakens the trees

Aphids

AFFECT
All fruit trees, although damage is most conspicuous on plums attacked by the leaf-curling aphid. In most years, the inevitable minor infestations may be tolerated but damage can be severe on young trees.

RECOGNITION
Usually, the first sign is the appearance on the leaves of sticky honeydew excreted by the insects but, on inspection, the green, grey, black, brown or yellow creatures themselves will be seen. There may be curling of the leaves and distortion of the shoots and, on plums, this can be quite dramatic. Attacks by woolly aphids on apples induce swelling and cracking of the bark in which small insect colonies form, covered in a waxy, white 'wool'.

POSSIBLE CONFUSION WITH
Apple canker and peach leaf curl. The presence of the insects is diagnostic but the secondary effects of the woolly aphid may be confused with the symptoms of apple canker.

NON-CHEMICAL TREATMENT
None, except cutting out branches badly infested with woolly aphids.

CHEMICAL TREATMENT
Apply tar oil when the trees are quite dormant in mid-winter to reduce the numbers of eggs and insects over-wintering on the bark. Also, spray young trees thoroughly with a contact insecticide immediately before and after flowering.

Pear leaf blister mite

Although attacks usually result only in yellowish leaf blisters that gradually darken as the season progresses, there may be more serious damage with distortion of the shoots and consequent reduction of the trees' vigour. As with most species of mite, control is difficult and the only really effective procedure is to collect up and burn the affected leaves. Composting the leaves will destroy the mites but only if the compost heap is functioning very efficiently.

Pear midge

Usually, the first sign of attack is the dropping of the young fruits in early summer. Unlike the normal 'June drop' of fruit, these fruitlets are dark-coloured and distorted and contain tiny, yellowish grubs. Pear midge can be very annoying as certain trees are attacked year after year and chemical treatment of the problem is difficult and unreliable. The most satisfactory procedure is to clear up and burn all the fallen fruitlets, and to rake derris insecticide dust into the soil under the trees to kill the insects.

Winter moths

AFFECT
All types of fruit tree and many ornamental trees and shrubs.

RECOGNITION
Leaves take on the holed, tattered and generally ragged appearance that is typical of caterpillar damage. The buds, shoots and blossoms are also attacked

Grease bands trap flightless female winter moths crawling up the trunk

and, on close inspection, the green or brown caterpillars will be seen, characteristically adopting an arched attitude called looping. Although the fruits aren't attacked directly the trees do suffer, after repeated attacks, through the indirect effects of loss of blossom and leaves.

POSSIBLE CONFUSION WITH
Other types of caterpillar which may occur on fruit trees from time to time. These are rarely of the looper type and are rarely present in the large numbers of winter moths.

NON-CHEMICAL TREATMENT
The best protective treatment for fruit trees is a band of grease which is applied in a complete band on the bark around the trunk about 10-12.5cm (4-5in) wide and 1-1.5m (3-5ft) above ground level. It's important to use grease specially manufactured for this purpose or to use the greased paper strips now available. Banding should be applied in mid-autumn, to prevent the flightless female moths from crawling up the trunk to lay their eggs.

CHEMICAL TREATMENT
A contact insecticide such as permethrin or derris can be sprayed on to the tree immediately after the buds have opened in spring, but may not be necessary if the grease band has been carefully applied.

RESISTANT VARIETIES
In my experience, no varieties of fruit tree display significant resistance and if there are insects in the vicinity and weather conditions suitable, they will cause damage.

Pest-damaged apples

Three types of pest damage are exceedingly common on apples and, although two of the pests can usually be found in the act of devouring the ripe fruit, the other only leaves characteristic signs of its activity. The number one pest is the codling moth, followed closely by apple sawflies with seldom-seen capsid bugs third.

RECOGNITION

Attack by codling moth larvae is difficult to detect externally because the small caterpillars normally burrow into the fruit through the 'eye' and are only discovered, together with the mangled tissues around them, when the apple is cut in half or bitten through. Sawfly larvae also tunnel into the fruit but they can often be detected externally as they cause characteristic, curved, surface scarring. Capsid bugs are rarely seen but leave typical bumps on the surface of the fruit and, quite commonly, tattered leaves also.

POSSIBLE CONFUSION WITH

Other pests and some physical factors may cause malformations that can resemble the surface damage caused by capsids and sawflies; but the internal damage by both sawflies and codling moth is quite distinctive.

NON-CHEMICAL TREATMENT

Sacking is often tied around the trunks in early summer to trap the codling moth larvae which pupate beneath it. However, it's of little real value as the damage will already have been done

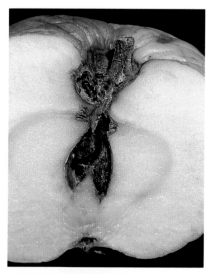

Codling moth damage is usually invisible until it is too late

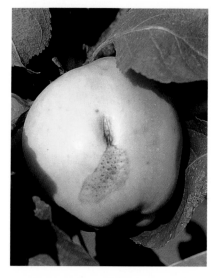

Capsid bugs cause rough scars but don't affect eating quality

and, the following year, female moths can fly in from neighbouring trees to lay eggs. It is better to use a pheromone-containing trap which is hung in the trees to lure males by using a chemical that simulates the sexual attractant of the female. Traps are available at garden centres or by mail order.

CHEMICAL TREATMENT

Capsid bugs don't warrant chemical control. Protective treatment to control sawfly and, more especially, codling moth, is worthwhile provided that the trees are small enough to make it practical. Spray with permethrin just after the petals have dropped, again when the fruitlets are the size of a small fingernail and again about 10 days later.

Bigger pests of fruit

The major problem bird among fruit crops is the bud-eating bullfinch which moves into gardens in small flocks in the winter. Although soft fruit can be adequately protected against bullfinches with netting or with a more permanent fruit cage, it's almost impossible to protect tree fruits. Several bird species also peck mature fruit and so create a wound which spoils any chance of their being stored. These damaged fruits must be removed before they decay and affect other, healthy fruit nearby. Wasps commonly follow after birds and enlarge the initial peck wounds but if the damaged fruit are removed promptly, the numbers of insects will be diminished. Only if a wasp's nest is in, or very close to, dwellings where children, or anyone with particularly severe allergic reactions to stings could be attacked, is eradication with chemicals justified. Never forget that, for much of the year, wasps feed on other insects, many of which are much more serious pests than the wasps themselves.

Brown rot

AFFECTS
All tree fruits, but generally most conspicuous and severe on apples and plums.

RECOGNITION
In most seasons, almost every tree will have at least a few fruit affected with characteristic brown decay, usually with more or less concentrically arranged whitish pustules of mould growth. The disease spreads very rapidly by contact between diseased and healthy fruit.

POSSIBLE CONFUSION WITH
Several other rotting diseases, such as *Botrytis* grey mould can affect fruit while they are still on the tree, but brown rot is by far the commonest and the concentric rings of pustules are characteristic.

NON-CHEMICAL TREATMENT
It's simply not possible to eliminate the risk of brown rot attack, especially on large trees, as decay usually begins where fruit have been damaged (by birds or insect pests for instance). Take special care with fruit needed for storage: reject any with any signs of damage, handle carefully to minimise bruising, never pull out the stalk, and promptly remove any stored fruit showing signs of decay.

CHEMICAL TREATMENT
No chemical treatment available.

RESISTANT VARIETIES
None.

Plum rust

AFFECTS
Plums and, to a lesser extent, peaches and almonds. Rust diseases aren't found on apple or pear trees in gardens.

RECOGNITION
Bright yellow spots on the leaves with dark brown or black, dusty patches beneath. In severe attacks, the leaves wither and drop.

TREATMENT
On large trees, no control is really feasible but if the trees are young and/or growing on a dwarfing rootstock, it may be worthwhile spraying them with a copper-containing fungicide, once when the fruit are half grown and after they have been picked.

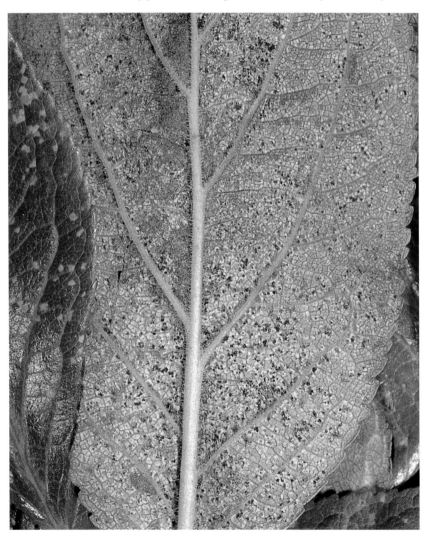

Plum rust can weaken young trees if attacks occur repeatedly

Canker

AFFECTS

All types of fruit tree, but the canker on apples and pears is quite different in cause, effect and treatment from that affecting plums and cherries. Many different types of ornamental tree may be affected by similar diseases and the comments below, relating to apple and pear canker, are equally applicable to them.

RECOGNITION

Sunken, more-or-less circular or elongated lesions develop on the branches or, sometimes, the main stems. These lesions extend slightly each season until, eventually, they may totally girdle the stem which dies beyond that point. Plum and cherry canker is somewhat different in form producing extensive cratering of the bark and long, sunken depressions exuding quantities of gum. Commonly the leaves of affected trees become holed or tattered.

POSSIBLE CONFUSION WITH

Mechanical wounds on trees although these tend to occur singly, unlike cankers which usually affect several parts of a tree, and often several different trees, simultaneously. Mechanical wounds don't, of course, extend annually. Plums and cherries often exude gum as a response to wounding but only when it occurs very extensively is canker likely to be the cause.

NON-CHEMICAL TREATMENT

Canker lesions must be cut out during the winter and burned; this is especially important where new trees are to be planted in a garden already containing diseased individuals. If the amount of cankering is severe then, regrettably, the trees should be destroyed; if you do keep them, perhaps because they look attractive, then don't be disappointed if your new trees become diseased too. On plums and cherries, where the lesions are more diffuse and where the causal organism is likely to be present throughout the tissues of the tree and not confined to the obviously damaged areas, felling and uprooting really does make sense.

CHEMICAL TREATMENT

No effective chemical treatment possible.

Canker lesions should be cut out

RESISTANT VARIETIES

All varieties of fruit trees are prone to cankering but if the garden or neighbourhood has a known history of the disease, then apple varieties such as 'Bramley's Seedling' or 'Newton Wonder', or some of the more modern types, which tend to be attacked less severely, are sensible choices.

Peach leaf curl

AFFECTS

Peaches, nectarines and, most seriously, almonds; but neither ornamental cherries nor plums.

RECOGNITION

Shortly after the young leaves unfold in

Act early to check leaf curl

spring, they become puckered and crumpled and soon become covered with a white powder. As the summer progresses, they gradually turn red then, finally, appear brown and shrivelled and may ultimately drop. If attacks develop repeatedly, the vigour of the tree will decline.

POSSIBLE CONFUSION WITH
Leaf-curling plum aphids. Although unlikely to be confused with other problems on peaches and almonds, similar leaf puckering can develop on plum trees as a result of infection by the leaf-curling plum aphid, which needs quite different treatment (see page 48).

NON-CHEMICAL TREATMENT
If the damaged leaves are collected from the tree during the early part of the season and burned, this will have some effect in diminishing the problem. Once the white 'bloom' has appeared, however, it really is too late for the spores will already have been shed. Trees trained against walls may be protected by a 'curtain' of plastic sheet during the critical infection period in early spring.

CHEMICAL TREATMENT
The best time to apply a spray is during the early spring, as the young buds are beginning to burst, followed by a second spray just after the leaves have dropped in the autumn. The most effective chemical is one containing copper but it must be appreciated that two or three years' treatment may be needed to master the problem on a badly affected tree. Trees growing in very moist sites may never be free of the problem.

Scab

AFFECTS
Apples and pears especially. Scab is the term used for diseases that result in a hard, crusty patchiness, although the scab disease that affects potatoes and root vegetables is a quite unrelated problem (see page 76).

RECOGNITION
Scab affects leaves, fruit and twigs, although twig symptoms are usually mistaken for tiny cankers. On the leaves, rounded, dark, dusty blotches form, while on the fruit the characteristic scabby lesions develop.

POSSIBLE CONFUSION WITH
Leaf spotting from various causes, but the combination of both fruit and foliar symptoms is diagnostic.

NON-CHEMICAL TREATMENT
As scab survives mainly on the leaves during the winter, these should be collected up and burned after an attack has occurred. Twig lesions should also be cut out if they are found.

CHEMICAL TREATMENT
Timing is important with spray treatments: they should be applied every two weeks from the time of bud burst until blossom fall, unless the disease is very severe, when the sprays need to be continued throughout the season. Carbendazim is the best chemical to use.

RESISTANT VARIETIES
Overall, more of the older apple varieties are scab-prone and this is a major reason why they fell from favour. In wet seasons, however, almost any type of apple and pear can be affected.

Scab is almost unavoidable on old pear trees and must be tolerated

Powdery mildew

AFFECTS
Almost all types of fruit tree and you are likely to see it on apples almost every season.

RECOGNITION
The dusty, white covering to leaves, shoots and other parts of the tree is familiar and unmistakable. A characteristic effect on apples is the shedding of all except the terminal tuft of leaves at the end of diseased shoots. On peaches, the symptoms quite commonly spread to the young fruit as well.

POSSIBLE CONFUSION WITH
Peach leaf curl (see page 52) which also causes powdery white growth; the puckering of the leaves, however, is quite unlike the effects of mildew.

NON-CHEMICAL TREATMENT
Pinch out the affected leaves and shoot tips on small trees as soon as they are seen in spring. On apples and pears, shoots affected in the previous season should also be cut out during the winter and burned.

CHEMICAL TREATMENT
Chemical treatment is a good idea on small trees in a season following a severe outbreak. Spray with carbendazim at the early pink bud stage and repeat fortnightly until midsummer. No other chemical is likely to have much effect; sulphur, once widely used, can damage some varieties. See page 88-89 for information on the correct stage of growth at which to spray.

Silver leaf causes silvery foliage and serious dying back on old trees

Silver leaf

AFFECTS
Plums, apples, cherries and many other trees and shrubs although it's always serious on plums, especially 'Victoria'.

RECOGNITION
A silvery sheen develops in the foliage as the leaf tissues separate and allow air to enter between them. The wood of affected branches has a brown stain within and, gradually, twigs, branches and entire trees may die back. The bark may bear flat, purplish fungal growths.

POSSIBLE CONFUSION WITH
False silver leaf. The silvery sheen to the leaves is distinctive but not unique, for similar symptoms can arise in false silver leaf, a nutritional disorder indicating a deficiency of fertilizer. Unlike silver leaf, there is no stain in the wood.

NON-CHEMICAL TREATMENT
Initially, do nothing as trees sometimes recover. Any branches cut off should be burned and, if the brown wood staining extends into the trunk, the indications are more serious. If suckers emerge with silvered leaves, the rootstock will certainly be diseased and the entire tree should be destroyed. Destroying the affected leaves is pointless as they don't contain the fungus.

CHEMICAL TREATMENT
No chemical treatment available.

RESISTANT VARIETIES
None. Gages and damsons tend to be affected least severely. Among other fruit trees, pears are rarely affected.

Viruses and certified planting stock

Gardeners used to be puzzled when fruit trees began to decline in vigour and fruiting as they aged and couldn't be revived by normal pest or disease control or fertilizer treatments. The cause is now known to be a build-up in the plants of viruses. It is possible artificially to free plants (or, at least, the 'parent' stock from which they are derived) from this viral contamination. Any reputable modern supplier of fruit trees will sell only virus-free stock and you should buy this whenever possible therefore. You can't be certain that a tree is declining because of virus contamination without eliminating all the other possibilities, although there may be tell-tale clues such as irregular, pale-coloured leaf patterns.

Stony pit virus symptoms on pear causing the fruit to appear lumpy

Blossom problems

The sight of a fruit tree in full blossom in spring should mean a bumper crop. Quite frequently, it doesn't. The reasons are sometimes apparent: perhaps there is no appropriate pollinator tree nearby, or perhaps there has been a late frost; but perhaps the cause is a blossom disease.

Blossom wilt

One form of this arises from the same cause as brown rot of fruit, but in this instance the disease fungus attacks the young flowers. Removing any diseased fruit from the tree is, therefore, doubly important; certainly none should be left hanging over winter.

Other problems

On pears, death of the blossoms is likely be the result of bacterial attack. The most serious is fireblight, which affects many tree and shrub members of the rose family and is consistently most damaging on pears (see page 44).

A small group of insects, descriptively named suckers live in and feed on the opening buds and blossoms (and, to some extent, the leaves) of apple and pear trees, causing distortion of the blossom and loss of the crop. Sucker infestations are usually accompanied by sticky, black masses of honeydew and sooty mould growth. Suckers can be controlled by chemical treatment: a tar oil winter wash will help to eradicate eggs overwintering on the bark.

SOFT FRUIT

"What kitchen garden is worthy of the name without some soft fruit canes and bushes in the summer? Unfortunately, the juiciness and succulence of the fruit appeals to other consumers too and, as a group, they have a disproportionate number of pests and diseases. The various soft fruit plants belong to two distinct families: strawberries, raspberries, blackberries and hybrid berries in one, and currants and gooseberries in the other. In consequence, they tend to suffer from a different range of problems, although some, such as mildew and aphids, are common to them all. As with tree fruits, the importance of starting with healthy stock can't be over-stressed, but as soft fruit have a much shorter life span, most gardeners are likely to make a soft fruit planting on average every few years while some may go for a lifetime and never need to plant new fruit trees."

Big bud

AFFECTS
Blackcurrants.

RECOGNITION
Some of the buds swell to an abnormal size early in the year and fail to open satisfactorily. The bud swelling is brought about by an infestation of minute creatures known as gall mites. But the secondary effects of gall mite attack are more insidious, for the mites can inject a virus into the plants which results in a gradual decline, a condition known as reversion.

Big bud symptoms at shoot tip – some buds are abnormally swollen

POSSIBLE CONFUSION WITH
Nothing.

NON-CHEMICAL TREATMENT
Remove and burn the affected buds promptly. If the attack is relatively slight, you may be able to eradicate an infestation in this way. Once a large number of buds regularly show the symptoms and the quantity and quality of fruit production declines, the only sensible action is to uproot and burn the bushes. Plant new stock as far away as possible from the site of diseased plants. In most gardens it's sensible to renew blackcurrant bushes every seven or eight years as a routine.

CHEMICAL TREATMENT
No chemical treatment available.

Caterpillars and similar pests

Although most types of plant will be attacked by caterpillars at certain times, gooseberries, currants and, in some areas, raspberries are the soft fruits most likely to be attacked.

Gooseberry sawfly larvae

The principal pests, by far, are the dingy green larvae of the gooseberry sawfly which can strip gooseberry and currant bushes bare of leaves almost in a trice.

Magpie moth caterpillars

The conspicuous black, yellow and white caterpillar of the magpie moth is another pest that causes similar damage and responds to similar treatment: spray with a contact insecticide such as permethrin immediately the first symptoms are seen.

Raspberry moth caterpillars

The caterpillars of the raspberry moth cause rather different damage: the tiny pink larvae tunnel into the young shoots causing them to wither and die. This pest is best combated by paying careful attention to garden hygiene by thoroughly removing damaged leaves and routinely pruning out old canes each season.

Raspberry beetles

These are among those garden pests that unfortunately become apparent too late: when the fruit are being prepared or, even worse, just as one is being popped into the mouth. The small, brownish grubs burrow into the ripening fruit so it's essential that insecticide sprays (fenitrothion is the most effective) are applied immediately after the petals have fallen and before the insects have penetrated.

Red spider mites

AFFECT
Strawberries are most likely to be affected among soft fruit but red spider mites also infest a wide range of other plants, especially in greenhouses (see page 78).

RECOGNITION
Red spider mites are exceedingly small, about 0.5mm (¹⁄₅₀in) long and more a dirty orange than red. First indications of an attack are usually a speckling, discolouration and withering of the leaves. Affected plants will be seen to be festooned with a cobweb-like covering on which the mites crawl. Rather larger, bright red coloured mites may often be seen in the garden. These aren't a cause for concern as they are not red spider mites and some types even prey on the pest species.

POSSIBLE CONFUSION WITH
Shrivelling of the leaves can be the result of water shortage or infection by disease but the characteristic minute cobwebs confirm red spider mite.

NON-CHEMICAL TREATMENT
Eradicating them physically is difficult because of their small size. My best advice, therefore, is to try to capitalise on their dislike of damp conditions: attacks are always worse in hot, dry seasons. Regular watering, the use of mulches and spraying the strawberry bed with water during warm and sunny weather are especially important. Spray as frequently as possible if infested plants are found but once the attack really gains a hold, it's unlikely that the damage can be arrested and you should then uproot and burn the plants and start afresh the following season.

CHEMICAL TREATMENT
As with all mites, treatment isn't easy as very few insecticides affect them.

Sawfly larvae can strip a gooseberry bush of foliage almost overnight

Aphids

As with almost every other species of garden plant, aphids of varying colours may infest all types of soft fruit, resulting in distorted leaves and shoots and possibly introducing virus contamination. It's worth giving your plants routine protection with a tar oil spray in winter while, in summer, you may also use almost any of the modern garden insecticide sprays, although care should be taken to follow the manufacturers' directions not to spray when the plants are flowering, as bees and other pollinating insects may be killed. Be especially careful with strawberries under polythene or glass as they are readily damaged by some chemicals particularly sulphur.

The rust fungus bursts out through tiny yellow slit lesions on the stems

Rust also causes leaf spotting

Rust

Among soft fruits, rust is seen most frequently on gooseberries and blackberries, although is it not one of the commonest diseases on either plant. The symptoms are, however, rather different: on gooseberries, orange-red pustules develop on the leaves and shoots and tiny craters or pock-like bodies form on these pustules during the summer. The leaves then become curled and puckered. On blackberries and related hybrid berries such as loganberries, reddish purple spots form on the leaves with yellow pustules beneath and yellow-orange, slit-like lesions on the canes. Damaged leaves and shoots should be cut out and burned and a protective spray with a copper-containing fungicide applied the following year, first as the young leaves unfold and then again just before the flowers open.

Leaf spots

AFFECT
Most types of soft fruit but in most instances the problem is not serious. It is important, therefore, to be able to identify the potentially damaging forms.

RECOGNITION
On currants and gooseberries, small, brown angular spots occur very commonly and their appearance is often followed by premature dropping of the leaves. On strawberries, variously sized brown or purple spots

are very common, although rarely accompanied by significant damage. On raspberries and related berries, purple spots may develop on both leaves and canes with consequent serious distortion of the canes and loss of fruit.

POSSIBLE CONFUSION WITH

Spotting of the foliage is a secondary symptom of a number of other problems, most notably some types of canker. Attack by insects can also cause leaf spotting but it is then usually accompanied by the presence of holes.

NON-CHEMICAL TREATMENT

Affected leaves should be collected and burned, as far as this is practicable. Damaged raspberry canes should similarly be destroyed.

CHEMICAL TREATMENT

After an attack has occurred, spray currants or gooseberries in the following season with carbendazim immediately after flowering and again two weeks later. Raspberries should be sprayed at the time of bud burst and again two weeks later. There are no satisfactory chemical treatments for leaf spotting on strawberries but, by and large, this is a problem that need cause no concern.

RESISTANT VARIETIES

If you grow the older raspberry varieties you will be especially likely to experience problems. The strawberries 'Cambridge Favourite', 'Redgauntlet' and, in my garden at least, 'Royal Sovereign' are also particularly prone to damage from leaf-spotting diseases. There are many modern varieties of soft fruit with high levels of resistance.

Grey mould

The grey mould *Botrytis*, appears in almost every section of the book for it is the ubiquitous pathogen, attacking and growing on all moribund or weakened plants, or the softest and most vulnerable of their tissues under damp, cool conditions. It affects all forms of soft fruit and is an especially serious cause of fruit decay on strawberries, raspberries, blackberries and related hybrid berries such as boysenberries, loganberries and tayberries. On gooseberries, it commonly causes die-back of the shoots.

The powdery, grey mould will be familiar to all gardeners and is unlikely to be confused with any other problem. The powdery growth of mildew, by contrast, is white, not grey, and tends to affect the parts of the plant on which grey mould is generally less severe – the leaves and shoots. Common sense

in your gardening will help minimise the effects of grey mould: bush and cane fruits should be adequately spaced and carefully pruned to avoid overcrowding (see Book 4 of this series, *Best Soft Fruit*) and strawberries should be mulched with bracken, straw or proprietary mats as the fruit ripen to minimise contact with the soil.

Ultimately, the likelihood of attacks developing depends on the weather so some chemical protection is wise. The most reliable chemical for grey mould control is carbendazim, which will help if applied immediately after the symptoms appear. Better, however, is a protective spray before damage occurs and, as the initial infection normally arises through the flowers, not directly on the fruit, the chemical should be applied shortly after the flowers open, with a repeat treatment about 10 days later. More organically minded gardeners may prefer to use sulphur, although I find it less effective.

Botrytis *grey mould spreads from one fruit to the others in contact*

Mildew

AFFECTS

All soft fruits to some degree but the symptoms on strawberries are rather different from those on currants and gooseberries. Raspberries aren't usually affected to any significant extent.

MOULD

On strawberries, the leaves tend to curl up at the edges before turning brown. Turning the leaves over will usually reveal at least a small amount of whitish mildew growth. The effects on raspberries, when they occur, are very much the same. On currants however, and, more seriously, gooseberries, a typical white, powdery covering forms on the leaves and young shoots, followed later in the season by a very characteristic brown, felty growth.

POSSIBLE CONFUSION WITH

Water shortage on strawberries, but no mould on undersides of leaves.

NON-CHEMICAL TREATMENT

Always take care to prune bushes regularly to ensure that good air circulation is maintained. Avoid any excessive use of nitrogen-rich fertilizers and never plant soft fruit in a shady part of the garden. Old strawberry foliage should be cut off and burned at the end of the season.

CHEMICAL TREATMENT

This may be necessary in dry years and the best fungicides to use are carbendazim or the mixture of bupirimate and triforine. Spray gooseberries as the flowers open, repeat after fruit set and again two weeks later. Currants should be sprayed as the flowers open and again every two weeks until midsummer.

Sulphur is sometimes recommended for strawberry mildew but can actually damage some varieties and I think it is probably better avoided. The modern fungicides are more reliable and can be applied as frequently as fortnightly after the first signs of disease are seen, but always take care to follow the manufacturers' directions regarding the minimum time interval between spraying and harvesting.

Viruses

In addition to the special case of reversion disease on blackcurrants (page 56), other types of soft fruit are also likely to be affected by virus contamination. In most instances, the symptoms are pretty obvious. On raspberries and blackberries, an irregular pattern of pale green or yellowish areas develops on the leaves (but don't confuse this with the very common and more uniform inter-veinal yellowing that occurs on alkaline soils and may be corrected by the application of sequestered iron). Blackberries may be markedly stunted with few fruit and weak, feeble canes. On gooseberries and currants, a pale yellow colour may develop on and around the leaf veins, while on strawberries, various forms of stunting, leaf malformation and irregular yellowing may occur with, occasionally and interestingly, the development of small, green flowers.

You can minimise all of these problems by paying careful attention to controlling aphids throughout the season as these are often responsible for virus being introduced into the

Gooseberry mildew is unusual in causing brown as well as greyish mould

One virus-like disease of strawberry causes strange green flowers

NON-CHEMICAL TREATMENT

Any damaged canes should be cut out and burned and careful attention paid to general husbandry, removing all old canes and thinning out new ones.

CHEMICAL TREATMENT

A routine spray with fenitrothion in late spring, repeated about two weeks later, will minimise the chances of cane midge attack. The routine early-season spraying with fungicide to prevent grey mould infection should help considerably to protect the plants against cane and spur blight also.

RESISTANT VARIETIES

Among popular raspberries, 'Malling Admiral' and 'Leo' have some resistance to spur blight whereas 'Malling Jewel' and 'Malling Promise' are particularly prone to midge attack.

stock. Once the symptoms develop severely, however, it is wise to uproot and burn the plants and replant, if possible, on a fresh site. You must obtain new stock from a reputable supplier and ensure that it is 'certified'. This will guarantee that it has been specifically produced to ensure that it is free from virus contamination at the time of purchase.

Problems affecting raspberry canes

Although raspberry canes may sometimes become spotted and distorted as a result of leaf spotting diseases (page 58), there's another group of specific cane problems that are partially interrelated and can cause rather serious damage. The three problems making up this group are cane midge, cane blight and spur blight.

RECOGNITION

Cracking of the bark is the most obvious symptom of cane midge attack and, during the summer and autumn, small pinkish maggots may be discovered feeding within these cracks. Very commonly, this type of damage is followed by infection with a fungus causing cane blight disease. Then blackened areas spread outwards from the cracks, the leaves shrivel and the canes die back rather pathetically. Spur blight tends to be a problem in cooler, more northerly areas and, like cane blight, may follow attack by the cane midge. Lengths of cane turn brown and the buds on affected parts die, resulting in a loss of fruit. During the winter, these cane lesions take on a very characteristic silvery colour.

POSSIBLE CONFUSION WITH

Physical damage to canes may cause lesions but on a much smaller scale.

Cane blight attack on raspberries

VEGETABLE FRUIT

"Vegetable fruit may be an unfamiliar term, but I find it a useful one, especially in relation to pests and diseases. They are the crops that are classified and grown as vegetables but which are cultivated for what, botanically, are their fruit rather than the leafy, vegetative growth or flowers. They include both greenhouse and outdoor tomatoes, cucumbers, marrows, courgettes and pumpkins, peppers and egg plants as well as peas, beans and sweet corn. They have in common the fact that many of the problems that occur on the fruit result from attacks on the plant at an earlier stage of growth, through the flowers. Most of the common problems associated with these crops are described here; the only major problem not considered is red spider mite, which can be very damaging and is described on page 57."

Black aphids may almost smother all parts of broad beans in the spring

Whiteflies are the worst pests of tomatoes and other vegetable fruits

Aphids

AFFECT
All vegetable fruit crops, both in greenhouses and outdoors. In greenhouses, tomatoes, cucumbers, peppers and eggplants are also likely to be affected by the consequent growth of sooty moulds on the honeydew secreted by the insects. Outdoors, broad beans are most commonly and severely affected.

RECOGNITION
There can be very few gardeners who are unable to recognise aphids. In greenhouses, the commonest species is the archetypal greenfly in varying shades of green. While the same or related species will also be found outdoors, it is the black species, known naturally enough, as blackfly that is probably the most serious pest causing severe stunting of young broad bean shoots.

POSSIBLE CONFUSION WITH
Nothing else, although the sooty mould growth that follows aphid infestation can also arise after whitefly attack.

NON-CHEMICAL TREATMENT
A jet of water will remove aphids from broad bean plants but it's rather chancy

with more flimsy types of plant and is certainly inadvisable in the greenhouse. Pinching out the young shoots before they become seriously infested early in the season can also be very effective. A biological control is available for greenhouse use (see page 12).

CHEMICAL TREATMENT

Fortunately, aphids can be controlled quite easily with almost any of the general garden insecticides.

Whiteflies

AFFECT

All the vegetable fruit crops in greenhouses; generally much less of a problem outdoors. Usually the commonest and most serious greenhouse pests, especially damaging to tomatoes.

RECOGNITION

Clouds of small, white, moth-like insects fly up when plants are disturbed; as they tend to congregate on the undersides of leaves, their presence is often not appreciated until the foliage is moved. As with aphids, the secondary effects of sooty mould growth are often considerably more significant than the direct damage caused by the insects.

NON-CHEMICAL TREATMENT

Biological control is available for greenhouse use (page 12) while the use of sticky yellow cards is an alternative and effective non-chemical remedy. It's important to replace the cards regularly during the summer and you should be aware that they will, of course, indiscriminately trap all insects, good and bad. Take care to inspect plants, such as fuchsias, that may be kept in the greenhouse over winter as the whiteflies can persist on them, ready to begin the first attacks of the new season.

CHEMICAL TREATMENT

Effective whitefly control with chemicals is extremely difficult because, while the adult insects are fairly susceptible to such products as permethrin or natural soap-based sprays, the immature forms are not. The key to success, therefore, is to be vigilant and repeat treatments every two or three weeks. Special care must be taken to spray non-systemic chemicals, like permethrin, thoroughly on the undersides of the leaves where the insects congregate.

Pea moth

AFFECTS

Only peas.

RECOGNITION

Unfortunately, the pea moth caterpillars aren't apparent to gardeners until it is much too late; usually the moment when the pods are being shelled in the kitchen and the tiny yellowish white larvae poke out their little black heads from holes in the peas and the pods are seen to be filled with a mass of chewed fragments. There is no damage to the leaves.

POSSIBLE CONFUSION WITH

Nothing else; the damage to the pods is diagnostic.

NON-CHEMICAL TREATMENT

Pea moth control isn't easy with chemicals so the cultural option should be considered seriously. The principle is to try and ensure that the flowers and young pods are not present when the female pea moths are laying their eggs early in midsummer. Choose carefully, therefore, those varieties that don't need to be sown in early and mid-spring. Sow either earlier or later.

CHEMICAL TREATMENT

Even if the sowing time is chosen extremely carefully, and even though chemicals aren't always entirely satisfactory, a spray with permethrin a few days after the first flowers appear, and again about two weeks later makes sound sense.

Pea moth results in useless pods

Leaf mould

AFFECTS
Tomatoes, mainly in greenhouses.

RECOGNITION
Distinctive yellowing patches on the leaves, with a brown or greyish mould on the undersides which may spread to affect entire leaves. In moist conditions, the foliage may drop and fruit production suffer.

POSSIBLE CONFUSION WITH
Botrytis grey mould and potato blight (see page 75); these may also affect tomato leaves but the latter is far more common on outdoor than greenhouse plants and neither disease produces the brownish mould.

NON-CHEMICAL TREATMENT
Good ventilation is the key to avoiding leaf mould infection; warm, humid and stagnant air in greenhouses must be avoided.

CHEMICAL TREATMENT
If attacks are spotted far enough in advance, spray at fortnightly intervals with carbendazim.

Botrytis grey mould

AFFECTS
All vegetable fruits if conditions are cool and damp, especially at flowering time, as the grey mould fungus commonly infects the developing fruit through the flowers.

RECOGNITION
The fruits of tomatoes, egg plants, cucumbers and marrows, and the pods of peas and beans all display fluffy, dark grey patches of mould, usually at the blossom end.

POSSIBLE CONFUSION WITH
Other causes of decay; although grey mould is the commonest, it's not the only problem causing fruit lesions or rot. Among others are potato blight which can affect tomatoes (page 75), blossom end rot (page 67) and soft rot (page 76). Rotting is also common on outdoor crops, the fruit or pods of which hang close to the soil; in this situation, it is best checked by covering the soil with a suitable mulch of straw or other material.

NON-CHEMICAL TREATMENT
I can't stress often enough that the control of grey mould relies on scrupulous attention to hygiene. Old plant debris must be cleared away promptly; dead or yellowed leaves should be removed from the lower parts of tomato stems and any affected fruit destroyed, and greenhouses must be well ventilated.

CHEMICAL TREATMENT
Carbendazim is the best fungicide to use and is particularly valuable because it may control other diseases on the same plants. Spray at the first sign of symptoms and repeat two weeks later.

Ghost spot

This is a mild symptom of attack by *Botrytis* grey mould and affects tomatoes either in unheated greenhouses or outdoors, especially as the weather cools towards the end of the season. Small, off-white, circular spots or rings form on the fruit, looking rather like the lime deposit that may form on the fruit if tap water is splashed on to them and allowed to dry but, unlike ghost spot, this can be wiped off. Ghost spot causes very little harm but improved ventilation may help limit it.

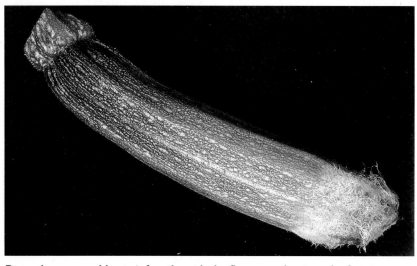

Botrytis grey mould may infect through the flowers and so into the fruit

Spots on beans

AFFECTS
Broad, dwarf and runner beans in different forms.

RECOGNITION
On broad beans, chocolate spot is the commonest disease, with rich brown lesions that spread rapidly, darken and eventually result in much of the plant becoming black and shrivelled. On dwarf and runner beans, especially in wet seasons, a red colour to the leaf veins on the undersides of the leaves and reddish spots on the pods are the signs of anthracnose disease, whereas more-or-less circular spots with pronounced yellow halos on the leaves and pods are the symptoms of halo blight. The small, powdery, brown pustules of rust may also sometimes be found on dwarf, runner and broad beans.

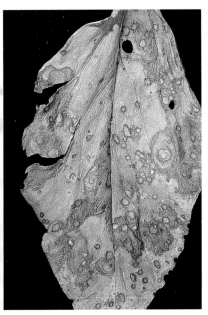

Three different bean leaf diseases

NON-CHEMICAL TREATMENT
Chocolate spot and, to a degree, the other diseases, can be minimised by not sowing broad beans too closely together, by not planting in the shade or on waterlogged soils and by not applying nitrogenous fertilizers.

CHEMICAL TREATMENT
Carbendazim, sprayed fortnightly, may go some way towards checking chocolate spot while copper-based fungicides may arrest the development of rust.

RESISTANT VARIETIES
Although varieties do vary in their susceptibility, there are none that I can recommend as resistant.

Sweet corn smut

This is one problem that gardeners may not see for years at a stretch. I know of some who have grown sweet corn for a gardening lifetime and never encountered it. When it does strike, however, usually in hot and dry summers, the effects are unforgettable: the young cobs develop in a grotesque, distorted fashion and the seeds 'explode' to spill out a black sooty mass of fungal spores. It is impossible to save the crop and the plants should be destroyed.

Powdery mildew

AFFECTS
Cucumbers, marrows, courgettes, pumpkins and also peas, although pea mildew is unable to spread to other types of plant.

Mildew on courgette leaves

RECOGNITION
A dusty, white covering to the leaves which soon become yellowed and tattered, and eventually wilt.

POSSIBLE CONFUSION WITH
Several factors can cause leaves to wilt, most notably a shortage of water in hot weather but the powdery, white growth is always diagnostic for mildew.

NON-CHEMICAL TREATMENT
In greenhouses, ensure adequate ventilation, although this makes it difficult to maintain the high humidity that cucumbers need.

CHEMICAL TREATMENT
Spray promptly with carbendazim and repeat two or three times at approximately 10-day intervals.

RESISTANT VARIETIES
There are no garden varieties that are reliably mildew resistant.

VEGETABLE FRUIT

LEAF PROBLEMS ON TOMATOES

Apart from the effects of leaf mould (see page 64) and potato blight (see page 75), which can cause mould growth on the leaves, tomato foliage very commonly shows other discolourations and malformations. Some of them are damaging, some not and so it's important to be able to differentiate the symptoms. In the table below, I've indicated the commonest of these symptoms, together with associated effects on other parts of the plants.

Symptom	Probable cause	Treatment/comment
Leaves, leaf stalks and stem twisted, thickened and distorted	Weedkiller damage	The usual source of the weedkiller is farmyard manure containing straw from treated cereal crops. In greenhouses, switch to ring culture or growing bags; outdoors, rest the site for one season
Leaves distorted and usually with yellowish blotches; fruit usually distorted also	Virus	Destroy plants; don't save seed from them and raise the next season's crop on different land (outdoors) or by ring culture or growing bags (greenhouse)
Leaves with rough, knobbly outgrowths on undersides	Oedema	Improve greenhouse ventilation
Leaves, especially those at the base of the plant, with pronounced yellowing between the veins	Magnesium deficiency	Ensure balanced tomato feed is used
Leaves curl upwards and become very dark green	Not a problem; a sign of good growth	None necessary

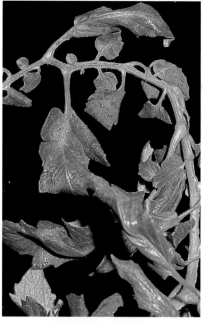

Weedkiller distorts the foliage

Basal rot on broad bean stems

Wilts and root rots

AFFECT
Tomatoes, peas and beans

RECOGNITION
An overall yellowing and stunting, usually with some dropping of the leaves and with blackening at the stem base and on the roots. Wilts are superficially similar but if the stem is split open 20-30cm (8-12in) above ground level, a characteristic brown staining will be seen.

POSSIBLE CONFUSION WITH
Anything that damages roots or starves plants of water, but the brown staining in the stem tissues is diagnostic.

NON-CHEMICAL TREATMENT
In greenhouses, switch to ring culture or growing bags. Outdoors, rest the soil for as long as possible from plants of the same type.

CHEMICAL TREATMENT

No chemical treatment available.

RESISTANT VARIETIES

Some tomato varieties that have been raised from seed have resistance to wilt and to some forms of root rot. Use these if space is limited outdoors and alternative land is not available; in greenhouses, ring culture or growing bags offer a far better solution.

Splitting, blackening and rotting

Two of the most common of all problems with tomatoes, splitting and blackening, arise as a result of fluctuations in the availability to the plant of water. It is impossible to emphasise enough how important a regular, steady water supply is to the tomato plant. If the plants have experienced a shortage of water when the fruit are ripening and are then watered steadily, the fruit will usually split. Some varieties are claimed to be less prone than others to such splitting but all are likely to be affected to some degree if they suffer a check in their water supply.

A shortage of water may also be followed by the development of hard, dark brown/black leathery patches on the developing fruit. This is called blossom end rot and is due to a shortage in the fruits of the element calcium, a condition exacerbated by dryness at the roots.

Decay of tomato fruit commonly follows fungal or bacterial infection. Mould growth may be present but the hard, brownish lesions of blight, commonly have no mould on them (see page 75). Other causes of decay are *Botrytis* (page 59) and soft rot (page 76).

Virus

AFFECTS

All kinds of vegetable fruit are affected by one or more types of virus. Generally, they aren't important on peas and beans, while virus problems on tomatoes are considered above. This leaves cucumbers and, to a lesser extent, marrows, courgettes and pumpkins which are all very commonly affected to some extent.

RECOGNITION

The leaves become crumpled or puckered appearance with irregular yellowish streaks and blotches. When the infection is severe, the plant as a whole is reduced in vigour.

POSSIBLE CONFUSION WITH

Pollinated fruit; the bitter-tasting fruit should not be confused with the bitterness that develops in some greenhouse cucumber varieties as a result of the female flowers having been allowed to become pollinated by the male flowers. Some fertilizer deficiencies may also give rise to leaf yellowing, but distortion is characteristic of virus.

NON-CHEMICAL TREATMENT

Attacks can be minimised but not eliminated by taking care over aphid control early in the season.

CHEMICAL TREATMENT

No chemical treatment available. Affected plants should be destroyed.

RESISTANT VARIETIES

Some varieties may be listed as having resistance but none is totally reliable.

Irregular watering very commonly causes splitting of the fruit

All kitchen garden plants have leaves, of course, but only in the group that I've called leafy vegetables do we eat them. The major plant family in the group is the Cruciferae which includes cabbages, cauliflowers, Brussels sprouts and the many increasingly popular Oriental vegetables (pests and diseases that have their principal effect on brassica roots will be found in the section that covers turnips and swedes (page 72). There are, however, leafy vegetables from other families too: lettuces, endives, spinach and the numerous spinach substitutes are the most important. And as the leafy parts of all of these plants are the object of cultivation, less leaf damage can be tolerated than with most other garden plants.

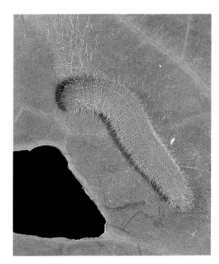

Caterpillar of the small white butterfly feeding on cabbage leaf

Caterpillars on leaves

AFFECT
Most vegetables, but the most important are butterfly and moth caterpillars on brassicas.

RECOGNITION
In severe attacks, the leaves are stripped and the caterpillars themselves are apparent. The black-and-yellow caterpillars of the large white butterfly are the commonest but the green larvae of the small white butterfly and the fat, green or brown ones of the cabbage moth can be equally damaging in some seasons. In less severe attacks, holes will be seen in the leaves, with the plants fouled by droppings.

POSSIBLE CONFUSION WITH
Nothing else.

NON-CHEMICAL TREATMENT
If the plot isn't large, prevent the butterflies from laying their eggs by covering the plants with lightweight horticultural net. Even without a cover, regular inspection enables the gardener to hand pick the pests or their tiny yellow egg masses before they reach damaging levels. A biological control is also available in the form of a bacterial spray (page 14).

CHEMICAL TREATMENT
Contact insecticides, like permethrin, are the best to use as crops can then be harvested soon after treatment.

Birds and rabbits

The birds that cause trouble among brassicas tend to be different species from those damaging fruit (see page 50) or seedlings (page 27). The leaf-eating wood pigeon is the most important although sometimes others, including partridges and collared doves may be troublesome. Rabbits are conveniently grouped with birds as they are large, voracious, appear in big numbers and are similarly difficult to control. Modern audible or visual scaring devices are generally no more effective than the traditional scarecrow, but are less attractive and often cause more disturbance to neighbours than to the pests, while chemical repellents are of very limited effectiveness. Ultimately, some form of physical barrier is needed in the shape of a small-mesh wire netting fence with a base buried at least 30cm (12in) deep or turned outwards 30cm over the soil surface at 90° to keep out rabbits or a net cover draped over supports to keep away pigeons.

Aphids

AFFECT
All types of leafy vegetables but the cabbage aphid is particularly troublesome.

RECOGNITION
All gardeners will be familiar with the appearance of aphids, but the commonest of those on brassicas are distinctively grey. They occur in masses on the heads and among the leaves and, although a heavy infestation can affect plant growth, more commonly the aphids are discovered deeply embedded in the tissues after the vegetable has been cooked. On lettuces, root aphid attack causes the plants to wilt; the white, root-infesting

Grey aphids attack all types of brassicas and result in much wastage

insects are only seen when the affected plants are pulled up.

POSSIBLE CONFUSION WITH
Nothing else.

NON-CHEMICAL TREATMENT
Surface infestations may be hosed off but this has no effect on brassica heads where the insects are likely to reside in inaccessible crannies.

CHEMICAL TREATMENT
Of little value, as surface-acting contact chemicals, such as permethrin will merely deal with insects on the outside of the leaves and not eradicate the insects deeply entrenched within.

RESISTANT VARIETIES
None, except in the special case of lettuces with resistance to root aphids, where the varieties, 'Avoncrisp' and 'Avondefiance' are very reliable.

Leaf miners

AFFECT
Brassicas, celery and beetroot, though almost every type of garden plant suffers from insect larvae that tunnel between the leaf tissues.

Celery leaf miner attack

RECOGNITION
Irregular, usually pale leaf markings that betray the tunnelling activities of the pests.

POSSIBLE CONFUSION WITH
Nothing else.

NON-CHEMICAL TREATMENT
Remove affected leaves as soon as they are seen and destroy them.

CHEMICAL TREATMENT
Because the pest is inside the leaf tissues, a systemic chemical would be effective but attacks are seldom serious enough to justify this.

Whiteflies

AFFECT
Brassicas.

RECOGNITION
Small, white, moth-like brassica whiteflies appear identical to those in greenhouses (see page 78) and, again, the secondary effects of sticky honeydew and black, sooty mould growth are very often more significant in spoiling the produce.

NON-CHEMICAL TREATMENT
As the brassica whiteflies, unlike greenhouse whiteflies, can survive outdoors during the winter, it is essential that old vegetable debris is cleared away.

CHEMICAL TREATMENT
Extremely difficult, and almost never justified. Some whiteflies must be tolerated.

Leaf spots

AFFECT
All leafy crops; each has its own type of leaf spot diseases but relatively few are serious.

RECOGNITION
Lesions vary greatly in size, shape and colour but the only important ones are dark spots on brassicas (if present in large numbers), pale spots with holes in the centre that sometimes arise on winter lettuce in cold, wet seasons; and masses of tiny brown spots on celery leaves.

The mould growth of downy mildew on lettuce is only beneath the leaves

POSSIBLE CONFUSION WITH
Downy mildew (see below), which produces an off-white mould growth on the undersides; slugs can cause holes in leaves but slime trails are usually present. Virus infection may also cause black spotting (see opposite).

NON-CHEMICAL TREATMENT
Clear away crop debris at the end of the season and, if you save seed from your own plants, never do so from any showing disease symptoms.

CHEMICAL TREATMENT
Not worthwhile.

Downy mildew

AFFECTS
Mainly Brassicas, lettuces and, occasionally, spinach, although it is impossible for downy mildew to be transferred from one type of plant to the other.

RECOGNITION
Dirty yellow or brownish, character-istically angular spots on the upper leaf surfaces gradually spread, causing large areas of leaf to die. There is usually an off-white mould growth on the underside of the lesions.

POSSIBLE CONFUSION WITH
Leaf spots, which may be similar but less angular in appearance and without any mould growth.

TREATMENT
Clear away crop debris; no effective chemical controls are available for garden use.

Botrytis grey mould

AFFECTS
All vegetables under damp and cool conditions when stressed or weakened. Most serious on lettuces; especially after attack by downy mildew.

RECOGNITION
Fluffy, grey mould growth covers the soft decomposing tissues of the leaves or head. Other rot-causing fungi and bacteria then help to reduce the plant to a worthless mass. Grey mould attacks lettuce stems, especially where they have been weakened by slugs or other pests and this results in the head falling over and shrivelling.

POSSIBLE CONFUSION WITH
Other rotting diseases, although the grey mould growth is characteristic.

NON-CHEMICAL TREATMENT
Avoid the main primary causes of damage (inadequate fertilizer over-watering, downy mildew and slugs.)

CHEMICAL TREATMENT
If the disease is persistently trouble-some, and especially if the season is cool and damp, spray seedlings with carbendazim and repeat the treatment every two to three weeks.

Powdery mildew

AFFECTS
Brassicas. There are many different types of powdery mildew fungi and cross-infection between different types of plant is unusual; nonetheless, all require similar conditions and therefore a severe attack in the flower garden means that the problem may be expected on vegetables too.

RECOGNITION
One of the most familiar of all garden diseases; a velvety, white coating appears over the leaves with consequent yellowing and general loss of vigour.

POSSIBLE CONFUSION WITH
Downy mildew (see opposite), but this is similar only in name, causing an increased number of discrete areas of dead tissue. A disease called white blister sometimes affects brassicas (especially cauliflowers and broccoli); it too causes discrete areas of whitish growth, but is almost always accompanied by severe distortion of the plant.

NON-CHEMICAL TREATMENT
Clear away debris on which the mildew fungus might persist.

CHEMICAL TREATMENT
Carbendazim is the most satisfactory treatment; the spray may need to be repeated every two or three weeks in hot dry summers. Many gardeners decide that the cost, time and effort are not worthwhile and that provided some produce is obtained, damaged parts can be cut away after harvest.

Virus

AFFECTS
All leafy vegetables but most serious on celery and brassicas.

RECOGNITION
The overall loss in vigour due to virus attack may not be immediately apparent but the tell-tale leaf symptoms of yellowing, puckering and, most characteristic of all, mosaic or mottled patterns of paler colour are readily seen. On brassicas, dark brown-black spots may occur.

POSSIBLE CONFUSION WITH
Aphid attack which may also cause leaf puckering, but when the infestation is severe enough to do this, the insects themselves will be readily apparent. The black spotting on brassicas is impossible to differentiate from leaf spots caused by fungus. The more regular looking mosaics and mottles are similar to some effects of nutrient deficiency, especially of magnesium or manganese, but such deficiencies tend to affect all plants in a plot, whereas a virus infection is likely to occur on scattered individuals only.

NON-CHEMICAL TREATMENT
It's important to remove crop debris promptly. This is particularly so with old plants that may remain standing over winter: not only is this an unsound practice generally, but it gives an opportunity for the virus to persist.

CHEMICAL TREATMENT
None available, but controlling the aphids which spread virus is important. This is a feature of most virus diseases and can't be over-stressed.

Mosaic virus brings about typical irregular patterning on the leaves

ROOT VEGETABLES

"With root vegetables, much of the damage occurs where you can't see it. It's very important, therefore, to be able to recognise what is taking place beneath the soil from symptoms on the above-ground parts. Wilting, an odd change of leaf colour, a general stunting or a dark stain spreading up the stem should arouse suspicion; but confirmation will almost always mean uprooting plants. Although my main concern in this section is damage to the roots themselves, do remember that many of the problems of leafy vegetables also affect root crops. I have extended my interpretation of the term 'root' to include potato tubers and onion bulbs."

Cabbage root fly attacks plants irregularly through the brassica bed

Cabbage root fly

AFFECTS
Turnips and swedes; also cabbages, cauliflowers, Brussels sprouts, wallflowers, stocks and most other plants of the family Cruciferae.

RECOGNITION
The plants appear stunted, often with a characteristic red-purple coloration to the leaves. The roots are eaten and tunnelled by white maggots and, if they are attacked in the early stages, they may become dry and shrivelled. In later attacks, the surfaces of turnips and swedes become disfigured and irregularly channelled.

POSSIBLE CONFUSION WITH
Clubroot (see page 74) results in similar above-ground effects but also causes severe galling of the roots. A shortage

of nitrogen fertilizer may also result in reddish, stunted plants, but there are then no maggots or root damage.

NON-CHEMICAL TREATMENT
Plants planted or sown in late spring are at the greatest risk, but a small felt collar placed around each transplant is an effective deterrent to the female flies which lay their eggs on the soil close to the stem base. Collars are available at garden shops and some are available impregnated with insecticide. One of the biological controls for vine weevil (see page 14) has some effect against cabbage root fly.

CHEMICAL TREATMENT
This is never wholly reliable, but insecticides containing pirimiphos-methyl may be mixed into the soil immediately after transplants are put

out. If attacks are detected sufficiently early, it may be possible to save plants by watering them with a spray strength solution of pirimiphos-methyl.

Flea beetles

AFFECT
Turnips, radishes and swedes, also broccoli and many of the Oriental brassicas; seedlings of other cruciferous plants; related species of beetle attack other garden plants.

RECOGNITION
Numerous minute holes in the cotyledons and leaves. Attacks are always worst in hot, dry weather when the adult beetles (2-3mm) may be clearly seen jumping on and around the affected plants.

POSSIBLE CONFUSION WITH
Superficially, severe attack by leaf spotting disease or very serious mildew.

NON-CHEMICAL TREATMENT
Clear away affected plants and crop debris promptly and try to ensure that plants don't dry out in hot weather.

CHEMICAL TREATMENT
Scatter derris dust around the emerging seedlings.

Flea beetle renders plants useless

Carrot flies

AFFECT
Carrots and, to a lesser extent, parsnips, parsley and celery.

RECOGNITION
Above-ground parts may be stunted and the leaves are characteristically reddened. The roots are tunnelled by small, whitish maggots.

POSSIBLE CONFUSION WITH
Other forms of root damage and some types of virus may cause the foliage to turn red, but no maggots are present.

NON-CHEMICAL TREATMENT
By delaying sowing until early summer, you may avoid the egg-laying period. Disturbing the carrot foliage releases an aroma that attracts the flies so sow sparingly to minimise thinning. Watering immediately after thinning will help to remove the aromatic chemicals. Horticultural fleece spread over the plants will prevent the flies from landing to lay their eggs and a barrier approximately 60cm (24in) high around the plants may deter the low-flying females. Don't leave carrots in the ground longer than necessary and don't store them in the ground if fly attacks have been experienced during the season.

CHEMICAL TREATMENT
No chemical treatments effective.

RESISTANT VARIETIES
'Sytan' and, most impressively, 'Fly Away'.

Carrot fly tunnels in the root

Eelworms

AFFECT
Many different types of plant, but among root vegetables, the attacks of cyst eelworm on potatoes cause the only serious problems.

RECOGNITION
Poor growth and yellowed foliage and, in a large plot of potatoes, there may be a discrete group of discoloured and stunted plants among healthy ones. The diagnostic symptom is only seen when the plants are dug: groups of minute white or yellowish marble-sized bodies on the roots.

POSSIBLE CONFUSION WITH
The below ground symptoms are diagnostic but yellowed foliage can arise for many reasons.

NON-CHEMICAL TREATMENT
Rotation of potato crops will help minimise attacks although, once damage has occurred, you should avoid growing potatoes (or tomatoes, which can also be attacked) on the site for at least six years.

CHEMICAL TREATMENT
No chemical treatment available.

RESISTANT VARIETIES
If land is infested with the species of eelworm that produces the tiny yellow bodies, 'Pentland Javelin' and 'Maris Piper' are probably the best early and maincrop potatoes respectively. Unfortunately, they aren't resistant to the species that produces the tiny white bodies.

Clubroot

AFFECTS

Turnips and swedes; also cabbages, cauliflowers, Brussels sprouts, wallflowers, stocks and other plants of the family Cruciferae. The above-ground parts may wilt and appear stunted and the leaves take on the red-purple tint that is often associated with root damage. In severe attacks, the plants may die but poor growth is the commoner effect. The roots bear swollen and distorted outgrowths (galls) which ultimately decay.

POSSIBLE CONFUSION WITH

Cabbage root fly (page 72) which has similar above-ground symptoms; turnip gall weevil causes galls which contain a small grub; hybridisation nodules look similar but are hard, harmless galls on some varieties of swede and turnip.

NON-CHEMICAL TREATMENT

Maintain a long rotation between brassica crops, although this, on its own, doesn't mean that the disease won't appear. Don't grow brassicas on water-logged soil and ensure, by liming in Autumn with garden lime, that the pH does not fall below 7. Be careful not to introduce clubroot into uncontaminated gardens; avoid buying plants unless you know the source is clubroot free, and if you borrow tools, ensure that they are well scrubbed with hot soapy water before use. To grow plants on badly contaminated land, raise each individually in a pot of compost and plant them out with the root ball intact.

CHEMICAL TREATMENT

Protect transplants by treating them with a proprietary root-dip based on thiophanate-methyl.

RESISTANT VARIETIES

None is wholly reliable but the swede 'Marian', the turnips 'Milan White' and 'Purple Top Milan' and the broccoli 'Trixie' may be less affected.

Onion white rot

AFFECTS

Onions, garlic, leeks, shallots, chives and related ornamental *Allium* species. Almost always the most severe attacks arise on spring onions.

RECOGNITION

Small groups of plants display yellow leaves and their growth is stunted. Sometimes, the plants fall over and a matted, cotton-wool-like growth envelops the bulb.

POSSIBLE CONFUSION WITH

Botrytis or onion fly, which may cause the leaves to turn yellow, but no cottony mould forms. Mould on onion bulbs in store is caused by neck rot (see page 85), which requires a different type of treatment.

Clubroot is one of the most depressing sights in the vegetable garden

White rot on salad onions – at first, there is more fluffy mould growth

NON-CHEMICAL TREATMENT

Maintain a three or four-year rotation of onion crops, if possible. Remove promptly any diseased plants found, together with several spadeful of the surrounding soil, especially if the disease hasn't appeared on the land previously. Contaminated material is best disposed of by deep burial. None of the treatments for white rot is entirely satisfactory and if the soil becomes really severely affected, then raising spring onions in confined, raised beds or in large pots may be the only possible solution.

CHEMICAL TREATMENT

Add fungicidal dust containing carbendazim to the drill before sowing as a preventive treatment, but don't expect complete control. Soak garlic cloves and shallot or onion sets for 30 minutes in spray-strength carbendazim before planting; this is especially important on clean land as white rot is very easily introduced on new bulbs.

Potato blight

AFFECTS
Potatoes and outdoor tomatoes.

RECOGNITION
The foliage bears very dark brown or black blotches, usually with a thin white mould on the undersides. In damp weather, these spread very rapidly until the bulk of the leaves and stems becomes a softened, black mass. The potato tubers bear brown surface lesions with a characteristic red brown speckling within. They are inedible.

POSSIBLE CONFUSION WITH
Grey mould. This may sometimes affect potato foliage, especially if it has been bruised by people walking between the rows, although it's much more limited in extent than blight. Other types of rot also affect the tubers but the red-brown colour of blight is characteristic.

NON-CHEMICAL TREATMENT
Never dump old potato tubers in gardens. If they are infected, the emerging sprouts will be diseased and blight will spread to the new crop. When old potato tops are composted, cut off any tubers and bury them separately.

CHEMICAL TREATMENT
In damp summers, and especially if there has been disease in the previous year, it makes sense to apply a fortnightly protective spray of mancozeb to potato and outdoor tomato crops, starting in midsummer. In hot, dry seasons, however, attacks are most unlikely to occur and the treatment is unnecessary. Wash treated tomatoes before eating.

RESISTANT VARIETIES
None; some varieties, including the ever popular 'King Edward', are especially susceptible.

The first signs of blight on the leaves lead eventually to rotten tubers

Common scab

AFFECTS
Potatoes, beetroot, swedes, turnips and radish.

RECOGNITION
Roots or tubers are more or less covered by rough, scab-like lesions, although vigour and yield are little affected. Scab is most severe on light, free-draining, alkaline soils; similar symptoms with potatoes on wet, heavy soils are the result of attack by powdery scab, a quite different disease.

POSSIBLE CONFUSION WITH
A relatively harmless problem known as skin spot might be confused with a mild attack of common scab, while severe attacks of powdery scab, in which outgrowths develop on potatoes in

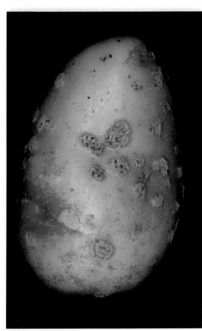

Common scab is usually tolerable

store, might be mistaken for the particularly serious, but now highly uncommon, wart disease.

NON-CHEMICAL TREATMENT
When attacks are light, the only problem is the inconvenience of the extra peeling. Nonetheless, to minimise damage, don't put scabby tubers on the compost heap, never lime soil on which crops have been attacked, instead dig in lawn mowings or other green matter. If attacks were quite severe in the previous season, water the crop as the tubers are swelling. Powdery scab is generally less common and more difficult to control; improving the drainage and a long rotation are the only practicable measures.

CHEMICAL TREATMENT
No chemical treatment available.

RESISTANT VARIETIES
Among varieties less prone to attack are 'King Edward', 'Pentland Crown' and 'Arran Pilot'.

Virus

AFFECTS
All root vegetables, but most important on potatoes.

RECOGNITION
A gradual decline, year by year, in crop vigour and yield if seed tubers are saved for replanting. Sometimes, there is upward rolling of the leaves (the lower leaves first), which often have a brittle texture, dark streaks along the leaf veins, or mottling or other pale green or yellowish patterns on the leaves.

POSSIBLE CONFUSION WITH
Little else; the leaf symptoms are unique, but it is important to remember that a poor crop can also be caused by inadequate feeding.

NON-CHEMICAL TREATMENT
Always buy new, certified seed tubers each season. These will have been grown in regions where virus-carrying aphids are sparse.

CHEMICAL TREATMENT
No chemical treatment available.

RESISTANT VARIETIES
Some, however, it is complicated as no potatoes are resistant to all viruses.

Soft rot (and black leg)

AFFECTS
All root vegetables, but probably commonest on swedes. Black leg is a potato disease that has much in common with soft rot.

RECOGNITION
Plant growth is stunted and, when pulled up, the roots or tubers have disintegrated into a foul-smelling, semi-liquid state; the outer skin may remain with the contents all but disappeared. Black leg on potatoes causes a black, slimy appearance to the stem base and inward rolling of the upper leaves.

POSSIBLE CONFUSION WITH
Few other garden diseases, although stored potatoes may have a number of similar problems.

NON-CHEMICAL TREATMENT

Don't plant potatoes or other root crops on land liable to water-logging and use only sound and healthy seed tubers. Over-applying manure or nitrogen fertilizer can predispose plants to soft rotting.

CHEMICAL TREATMENT

As with most bacterial diseases, there is no chemical treatment available.

RESISTANT VARIETIES:

The variety 'King Edward' tends to be less prone to attack by black leg.

Parsnip canker

AFFECTS

Parsnips.

RECOGNITION

Symptoms vary and you may see a purple-black decay that spreads from the small lateral roots, large purple lesions with a soft colourless margin, or rough orange-brown patches round the shoulder of the root.

POSSIBLE CONFUSION WITH

Other root-rotting problems, especially soft rot where the entire root becomes soft and squashy.

NON-CHEMICAL TREATMENT

Try to maintain a four-year rotation between parsnip crops. Earth up parsnips in summer to prevent the fungus from reaching the roots, and try sowing later than is recommended to produce smaller roots, which are less prone to attack. Always avoid growing crops on water-logged ground.

Orange brown canker on the crown

CHEMICAL TREATMENT

No chemical treatment available.

RESISTANT VARIETIES

'Avonresister' is unaffected by any of the forms of parsnip canker.

Misshapen roots

Badly formed roots, with no apparent pest or disease cause, are very frequent on carrots and parsnips. Commonest of all is the development of bifurcations or forks, generally known as fanging. There are four usual causes. First, fresh farmyard manure has been applied too close to sowing time; the land shouldn't be manured closer than just before the preceding crop. Second, the crop is on unsuitable land; the soil must be free-draining and of a fine tilth with no large clods or stones to impede root growth. Third, there is a 'pan' or hard layer several centimetres beneath the soil surface; deep cultivation will break this up. Fourth, the plants have been disturbed, generally during thinning.

Sometimes carrot roots split vertically. Like the splitting of tomatoes, cabbage heads, apples and other produce, this usually results from renewed growth following a dry period. It can be avoided by ensuring that the plants are always watered regularly and uniformly.

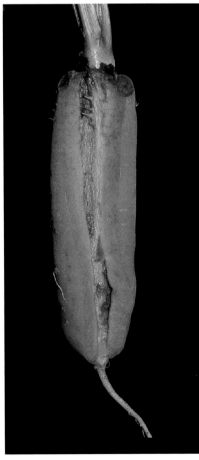

Dry summers often mean splitting

GREENHOUSE PROBLEMS

" The greenhouse offers a very different environment from the rest of the garden in the protection, warmth and general cossetting that it provides for our plants. Unfortunately, it provides these benefits for pests and diseases too; all-year round plants can suffer from all-year-round aphids and mildew. Similarly, in keeping exotic and tender plants, we are also providing conditions for exotic and tender pests that wouldn't stand a chance outside. It is important, therefore, to pay special attention to general hygiene in the greenhouse and make up for the natural, seasonal check to pest and disease development that the winter would normally provide.

Among the pests and diseases that occur in greenhouses, but are very troublesome outdoors too, are aphids, caterpillars, earwigs, thrips and woodlice among pests, with Botrytis *grey mould, damping-off, mildew, soft rot, sooty moulds and viruses among the diseases. Advice on these will be found in earlier sections of the book. More specific problems of indoor plants (some of which occur on house plants, too) are fungus gnats, mealy bugs and scale insects, while leaf-attacking moulds, red spider mites and whiteflies are almost always more serious in greenhouses than elsewhere. Therefore, I am offering some general guidance on green-house design and management to help maintain healthy plants. Trouble can be minimised by giving adequate thought to matters before purchasing your greenhouse. "*

Choosing your greenhouse

An enormous range of greenhouse styles is now available, but I am convinced that the most important factor in preventing the spread of pests and diseases is the effectiveness of the ventilation. Damp, stagnant air, especially at floor level, is an invitation to rot and decay so, when buying a new greenhouse, pay particular attention to the presence of vents low down, as well as in the roof. Constructional material is important, too, and it's sometimes said that wooden green-houses are more difficult to clean and disinfect as they contain more nooks and crannies. This isn't necessarily true; it is the thoroughness with which the structure is cleaned that matters and, indeed, aluminium greenhouses have the disadvantage that the metal framework may be damaged if sulphur fumigant candles are used to kill fungal spores in them.

Management of your greenhouse

Cleanliness is the prerequisite of health in the greenhouse and a sound routine of annual disinfection is essential. This must be done when the greenhouse is empty of plants – the most convenient time is generally in the autumn when large, immovable crops like tomatoes and cucumbers are finished for the season, but when the weather is still warm so the perennial occupants won't suffer from being placed outside for a few days. If your plants are in pots, the

The sticky card pest trap is essential and will collect hundreds of whiteflies

operation is better done in late summer. The entire fabric of the house and staging should be washed thoroughly with soap, water and a proprietary disinfectant.

Cleanliness means more than this, however. I must stress the importance of watching for the first signs of pest or disease and applying the appropriate treatment promptly. Make use of smoke or fumigant formulations of fungicides and insecticides whenever possible but remember that the vents and door must be closed and the entire structure must be air-tight for the technique to work effectively. It's equally important to be scrupulous in removing dead leaves and flower heads; not simply as a matter of tidiness, but because such dead tissues are breeding

78

grounds for problems like the grey mould fungus, *Botrytis*, which will rapidly spread from them to healthy plants.

Water is a vital greenhouse commodity and many gardeners have a rain-water butt to collect water from the roof. Be cautious when using this water in the greenhouse, however, for the warm conditions may incubate any pest or disease organisms that it contains and cause them to multiply to damaging levels. If you use rain-water in this way, cover the butt with a close-fitting lid and scrub out once a season.

Not only do greenhouse plants need water; they need to be fed too, but here also, a word of caution. Never use farmyard manure on tomato or cucumber plants as the straw that it contains may well have derived from cereal crops that have been sprayed with weed-killer. Even in minute amounts, this can cause the plants to distort, making them worthless. Be careful, too, when using the border soil in a greenhouse. While many gardeners now grow greenhouse crops in containers of various sorts, some still use the original soil. This is usually safe with crops such as lettuce, but is tempting fate with tomatoes as the fungi that cause tomato wilt can easily build up with repeated cropping and, once present, are almost impossible to eradicate. A switch to container production or, even to using grafted tomatoes with a wilt-resistant root-stock is then the only solution. Finally, smokers should desist from the habit in the greenhouse and wash their hands before touching plants, for cigarette tobacco may contain a strain of tobacco virus that can be spread by fingers to plants such as tomatoes.

Ring culture is a reliable and trouble-free method of growing tomatoes

GREENHOUSE PROBLEMS

1. Tight-fitting door to prevent escape of fumigant vapours and keep out mice or other pests.

2. The glass panes of the greenhouse must be kept clean; not only will they harbour potential disease organisms if allowed to become dirty but, in obstructing the light, they may place plants under stress in winter when some additional light will inevitably be filtered by the insulation sheet. Conversely, in summer, shading should be used, at least on the sunniest side, to prevent similar stress.

3. Tight-fitting roof ventilators, capable of being opened at least to 45 degrees to the horizontal. These act with the base ventilators to permit through-flow of air and prevent diseases from developing in stagnant conditions. The tight fit is essential to prevent leaking of fumigant vapours. The total area of opening ventilators should equate to at least 15 per cent of the greenhouse floor area.

4. Slatted benches for ease of cleaning. Once a year, the entire house should be cleared and disinfected thoroughly.

5. Basal ventilators. These are often overlooked but they are necessary to prevent the build-up of stagnant air at floor level, which will lead to stem and leaf rotting-problems.

6. Pot plants on the bench. Almost inevitably, the greenhouse will be used for raising a wide variety of different types of plant, some requiring more shade and less humidity than others. Do ensure that plants are placed

within the greenhouse in the most beneficial position.

7. Pots and plant containers must always be scrubbed and disinfected after use. This is especially important if they are to be stored in the greenhouse where any pests or diseases that they harbour may be spread to growing plants.

8. Gravel floor to the greenhouse to permit excess water to drain away easily. Although it might be thought that a concrete floor is more easily cleaned, it is much less versatile, and also extremely tiring to stand on for long periods if you are working at the greenhouse bench. An occasional watering of the gravel with a garden disinfectant will kill off any pests, diseases or weed seedlings.

9. Butt for rain water. This must have a tight-fitting lid to prevent algal and other growth from building up within. Because of the warmth within the greenhouse, which will incubate any pest or disease organisms, it is sensible to use water from rain butts outdoors only and to use tap water within the greenhouse itself.

10. Ring-culture bed for tomatoes or other crops. This is a more reliable way of raising these plants than in the border soil of the greenhouse where wilt and rot-causing fungi will almost certainly build up after a few crops.

* For clarification, some of the glazing bars have been omitted from the greenhouse illustration.

81

STORING FRUIT AND VEGETABLES

" Few things in gardening are more disheartening than to see a bumper kitchen-garden crop safely collected and put into store, only to be lost through rot, decay or pest activity in the ensuing weeks. In most cases, by the time that the damage is found, it is too late to do very much about it, other than learn from the experience. In this section of the book, therefore, I haven't described most of the problems in detail but have given general guidelines on the handling of produce intended for store and also on the conditions under which storage should be made. In the appropriate fruit and vegetable sections elsewhere in the book, you will find details of those pest and disease problems that occur while the plants are still growing, but which can compound storage difficulties if allowed to go unchecked. There is one exception, however, neck rot of onions, which is uniquely different from other storage problems and is described on page 85. Although this part of the book is concerned primarily with edible produce, much of what is said here is equally applicable to the stored bulbs, corms and tubers of ornamentals. "

One rotten apple can soon spread the decay to others so must be removed

Careful handling means less damage

In commercial growing, there has been a dramatic increase in recent years of losses through decay of fruit and vegetables in storage. This is due to the gradual phasing out of labour-intensive picking and sorting by hand in favour of mechanical harvesting and grading machines. There is a lesson to be learned here for gardeners because, although undoubtedly quicker than mere people, these extraordinarily ingenious devices don't possess the gentle touch that the slow old human hand affords. They bump and they bruise, they remove small pieces of skin or peel and they knock off immature buds; and nothing so predisposes fruit and vegetables to decay, because these wounds provide the entry points for fungi and bacteria to infect and the starting places for pests to nibble. If there is one golden rule, it must be that any garden produce intended for long or even short term storage must be collected and handled with the greatest care.

Checklist for efficient crop storage

■ Don't store windfall apples or pears; they will inevitably be bruised, even if you can't see any damage.

■ Don't drop any fruit that is to be stored, either on to the ground or even into the collecting basket; this too will bruise it.

■ Don't pull the stalk from fruit that is to be stored; this will cause quite sufficient wounding for infection to occur.

■ If vegetables have to be washed before storage, do this with the greatest care; ensure that they are well dried afterwards, but don't do this by exposing them to any form of heat, including the sun.

■ Don't attempt to store any produce that already shows the merest sign of pest or disease attack.

■ Grade your crops for size; smaller fruit and vegetables commonly keep better and longer than larger ones.

■ Ensure that bulbs or corms lifted from the ground for storage are well dried by arranging them on slatted trays in a well-ventilated shed or outhouse. Carefully rub away any dry soil and dead leaves and then reject any showing disease or pest blemishes.

■ Always harvest produce when it is at, or just below the peak of maturity.

■ Remember that some vegetables (carrots, beetroot and swedes, for instance) may be better left where they are, to be stored in the ground, with straw or other covering as frost protection.

■ If vegetables have to be trimmed or cut (to remove leaves, for instance) always do this with a clean knife.

■ If you intend to grow crops specifically for storing, always choose varieties listed in catalogues as suitable for this purpose. Some, for example, have very much thicker skins than others. Even a pin-prick hole can allow decay-causing fungi to enter and lead to damage out of all proportion to the initial wound.

Allow potatoes to dry for a short time before storing them in paper sacks

Ornamental bulbs, but not edible ones, may be dusted with fungicide

83

STORAGE CONDITIONS

Even if crops have been harvested and selected carefully, you may still lose your produce simply through neglecting the way in which they are placed in the store and, indeed, any problems with the nature of the storage place itself. The storage building should preferably be one that isn't subject to frequent disturbance (with people constantly going in and out, for instance), as this will lead to wide fluctuations in temperature and humidity. A garden shed is normally suitable, but garages or other buildings where toxic fumes might taint the produce are much less effective. If possible, install extra ventilators close to ground level and don't stack bags or trays of fruit and vegetables against the cold, shaded wall. Try to ensure that the building is rodent proof; in some years, wood mice and voles reach almost plague proportions and invade fruit and vegetable stores, gaining access through the smallest holes. There are, of course, optimal conditions for each and every type of produce, but in the illustration, I've indicated how crops harvested from a vegetable and fruit garden might be stored in a small shed.

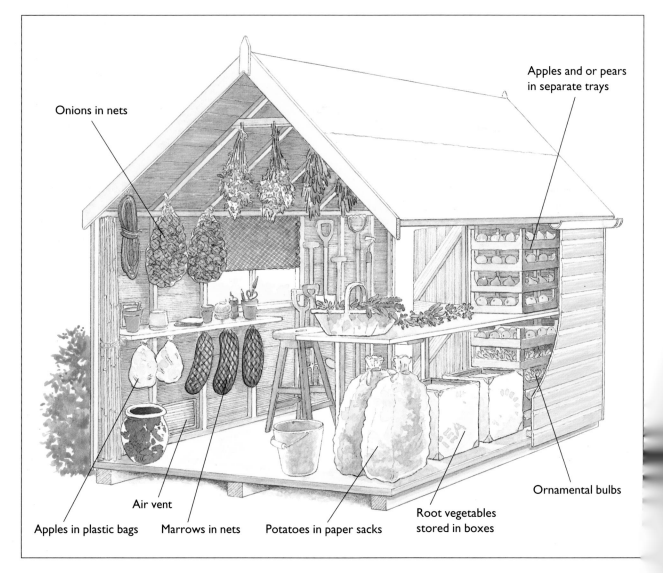

Onions in nets

Apples and or pears in separate trays

Ornamental bulbs

Air vent

Apples in plastic bags

Marrows in nets

Potatoes in paper sacks

Root vegetables stored in boxes

How to store produce most effectively

1. Store each type of fruit or vegetable separately.

2. Store apples, a dozen at a time, in clean plastic bags with tiny holes for ventilation.

3. Store pears individually on slatted trays.

4. Store potatoes in paper sacks, preferably of double thickness, and covered with insulation against frost.

5. Store onions, ornamental bulbs and large produce, such as marrows and pumpkins, separated on slatted trays or hung in nets.

6. Root vegetables are best stored in the ground in all except the very coldest areas, but where this isn't done or isn't practicable, they should be placed in layers in well-ventilated wooden boxes with sand between each layer.

7. The golden rule is to try and store produce somewhere that is well ventilated but, at the same time, not subject to disturbance from people regularly going to and fro.

Onion neck rot

AFFECTS
Onions and shallots.

RECOGNITION
The neck of the bulb softens and a grey-green mould growth gradually spreads down to affect the entire bulb which becomes brown and worthless.

POSSIBLE CONFUSION WITH
Superficially similar decay may occur on many types of vegetables and fruit in store but you should appreciate that onion neck rot is very different from all other conditions in that, although it can't be cured, its occurrence may be prevented by the most simple and improbable of methods.

NON-CHEMICAL TREATMENT
Don't dump old onions in the garden but bury them deeply in the compost heap or bag them up for disposal elsewhere. It's sometimes said that if you don't break the necks of onions before lifting, this will prevent neck rot from occurring. In practice, it makes almost no difference as any infection will almost certainly already be present in the plant.

CHEMICAL TREATMENT
The fungus responsible for onion neck rot has its origin on the onion seed and it grows quite invisibly on the onion while it is maturing in the garden. The treatment required to prevent the problem, therefore, is to dust the seed with carbendazim before sowing. Sets should be soaked in spray-strength chemical for about 30 minutes as described for ornamental bulbs.

RESISTANT VARIETIES
Although research has been carried out, no onion varieties have proved adequate resistance to neck rot.

Neck rot develops only in store, but originates on the seed

PEST AND DISEASE SPRAYING CALENDAR

"Even the most experienced gardeners need a memory jogger, a personal diary to remind them when to begin sowing their peas, the latest date at which weedkiller should be put on the lawn and so forth. This is especially true with pests and diseases where it's often important to catch the organisms at certain critical stages of their individual life cycle in order for control or avoidance measures to work effectively. The following calendar provides guidelines for combating most of the major garden problems mentioned in the book, with the exception of routine spraying of fruit trees which I shall come to in a moment. Not every gardener, of course, will need to make use of all the recommendations provided but even those who eschew the use of chemicals, either artificial or natural will, I hope, find some suggestions of value in helping with pest and disease avoidance.

The use of chemicals for the routine spraying of fruit trees in spring and summer requires the treatments to be applied at critical times. This is not only so the pest or disease is caught at its most vulnerable stage, but also in order to avoid the possibility of damage to the plants themselves or to beneficial insects and other wildlife. These timings are identified in relation to the growth stages of the fruit trees. As these vary, not only across the country, but also between varieties and seasons, they are shown pictorially on the next page and these illustrations should be used in conjunction with the chemical manufacturers' guidelines."

Pest and disease controls through the seasons

MID-WINTER

Clear away garden rubbish.
Look out for signs of coral spot on old branches and twigs.
Final chance to use tar oil winter washes on dormant woody plants.

LATE WINTER

First sprays for peach leaf curl as the buds are swelling.
Check that all pots, boxes, and seed trays are clean and disinfected.
Check for big bud symptoms on blackcurrants.
Check under old seed boxes and pots for woodlice and apply control measures.

EARLY SPRING

Second spray for peach leaf curl as leaves expand.
*Begin to use chemical and physical slug controls as first plants are put out.
Look out for, and pick off, the first signs of mildew as fruit tree leaves unfold.

MID-SPRING

*Begin to check routinely for aphids and whiteflies in greenhouses and put up sticky yellow cards.
*Protect brassica seedlings against flea beetle.
*Protect brassica transplants against clubroot.
*Use soil insecticides when pricking out young plants.
First spray on raspberries against grey mould.
Begin to apply predator and parasite based biological controls in greenhouses.

LATE SPRING

Protect brassica transplants against cabbage root fly.

*Check for caterpillars on all types of fruit, vegetables and ornamentals.

Begin sprays against raspberry cane midge.

*Check routinely for aphids on all types of fruit, vegetables and ornamentals.

*Begin sprays against rose mildew, black spot and rust.

Begin to apply nematode-based biological control measures outdoors.

Put up codling moth traps in fruit trees.

EARLY SUMMER

Spray for pea moth control before and after flowers open.

Carefully check over bulbs for pests and diseases after lifting and drying for storage.

MID-SUMMER

Begin protective sprays against potato blight in damp seasons.

Replace sticky yellow cards in greenhouses.

LATE SUMMER

Check that fruit and vegetable stores are rodent proof.

Replace sticky yellow cards in greenhouses.

Place earwig traps among dahlias and chrysanthemums.

Use sheeting to trap leatherjacket larvae on lawns.

EARLY AUTUMN

Check carefully all fruit intended for storage.

Soak bulbs in fungicide before planting.

MID-AUTUMN

Last spray against peach leaf curl as leaves drop.

Apply grease bands to fruit trees to control winter moth.

*Check stored fruit and vegetables and remove any that are damaged.

LATE AUTUMN

Remove dead wood from trees and shrubs; check for and cut out any cankers.

Take care not to cut too close to the trunk (see page 42).

EARLY WINTER

Apply tar oil winter wash or spray on dormant fruit trees for control of aphids and other pests overwintering in the bark.

* All the items on the calendar identified with an asterisk should be continued routinely, either every two or three weeks, or as and when symptoms reappear throughout the summer. Details of the best chemicals to use in each case are given in the main text throughout the book.

Spray programme for fruit trees

This spray programme is for apples, pears and plums, for the control of winter moths, codling moths, woolly aphids, aphids, sawflies, capsid bugs, suckers, scab and mildew; but do check the text for recommended chemicals in each case. Growth stages of fruit trees can be used to identify the correct time to apply sprays (note: winter washes should be used also, in the dormant season).

Bud burst
winter moth, aphids, scab

Green cluster
aphids, suckers, scab
(omit with plums)

Pink bud (or white bud on plums and pears)
mildew, scab

Petal drop
sawflies, codling moths,
capsid bugs, mildew, scab

Fruitlet
mildew, suckers (pears only),
codling moths, aphids (omit
with plums)

Young fruit
mildew, codling moths

NUTRITIONAL DISORDERS

All plants need feeding, and a fertilizer is essential to supplement the nutrients present in the soil or compost in which they are growing. For some plants, almost any additional feeding, no matter how irregular, will be adequate and they will never display the signs of shortage. Seedlings and bedding plants, for example, grow so rapidly and are so short-lived that they don't have time to develop the specific symptoms associated with the shortage of particular chemicals. This isn't true, however, of the remaining plants described in the book. The perennials, by definition, grow for a long time and can easily exhaust the available nutrient. This is even true of trees, especially fruit trees, which have to 'work hard' during their lives to produce their crops. Vegetables, although annual or biennial, put on so much growth in such a short time that they too can easily exhaust what is available. Although I've made no attempt in this book to give guidelines on general fertilizer use, I do think it important to recognise the commoner signs of nutrient deficiency, if only to be able to distinguish these from genuine pest or disease problems. The chart should help you to identify the commonest symptoms.

On LEAVES

What to look for	Plants commonly affected	Deficiency	Possible confusion with
Pale coloured, often with tints of purple, red or yellow. The leaves are generally small and the whole plant may appear stunted. Effects appear first on the older leaves and spread upwards	Brassicas and other leafy vegetables	Nitrogen	Root fly or club root; check that roots aren't damaged
Generally dull blue-green, sometimes with a hint of purple but not red or yellow. Older leaves are affected first and tend to be rather small; they may drop prematurely. Blackcurrant leaves become bronze	Many different crops	Phosphorus	Root fly or club root – check that roots aren't damaged
Edges appear curled and brown or scorched, while brown spots may develop on the undersides. The older leaves are affected first	Leafy vegetables, beans, tomatoes, potatoes and many fruits	Potassium	Cold or drying winds; salt spray at the seaside
Tips of young leaves curled inwards and ragged or scorched. Central leaves of celery crowns are blackened	Lettuces, celery, chicory	Calcium	Grey mould or boron deficiency

What to look for	Plants commonly affected	Deficiency	Possible confusion with
Yellow between veins giving a marbled effect. Plants with red leaves may turn irregularly purple. Older leaves affected first	Apples, tomatoes, brassicas, lettuce	Magnesium	Iron deficiency
Bleached or yellow with veins remaining dark green. Youngest leaves affected first	Rhododendrons, roses, camellias, hydrangeas, raspberries	Iron	Magnesium deficiency
Yellow between veins of older leaves, often with dead patches too. Younger leaves more generally yellow and sometimes rolled upwards. Peas and beans have brown blotches if the seed leaves are pulled apart on the germinating seed	Beetroot, peas, beans, parsnips, brassicas, potatoes, spinach, fruit trees and bushes	Manganese	Several other problems, but manganese deficiency is most likely on wet, organic soils
Leaves with imperfectly developed blade, giving a 'whip-tail' effect	Cauliflowers	Molybdenum	None

On FRUIT

What to look for	Plants commonly affected	Deficiency	Possible confusion with
Fruit small and highly coloured, combined with pale coloured leaves	Apple	Nitrogen	None
Fruit ripen unevenly, some patches remaining green	Tomatoes	Potassium	Virus, but then patchy while still green
Dark spots within flesh and on skin ('bitter pit')	Apples	Calcium	None
Dark brown, tough patch at blossom end	Tomatoes, peppers	Calcium	None

NUTRITIONAL DISORDERS

On VEGETABLES

What to look for	Plants commonly affected	Deficiency	Possible confusion with
Masses of small tubers	Potatoes	Nitrogen	Calcium deficiency, but this also produces 'leggy' shoots
Sprout buttons with dark internal patches	Brussels sprouts	Calcium	None
Roots with black patches and rings in flesh	Swedes, beetroot and turnip	Boron	Similar effects on potato tubers are caused by cold or virus
Curds with brownish patches	Cauliflower	Boron	None
Leaf stalks cracked and pithy	Celery	Boron	Water shortage

How to correct deficiencies

NITROGEN: Apply nitrogen-containing fertilizers and manures regularly every season before planting in spring. For very rapid response, use a liquid feed or a fast-acting nitrogen source such as dried blood or ammonium sulphate.

PHOSPHORUS: If balanced NPK fertilizers (general garden fertilizers containing Nitrogen, Phosphate and Potash) don't do the trick, apply superphosphate close to seeds or young plants.

POTASSIUM: If phosphorus and nitrogen levels are adequate, apply sulphate of potash before sowing. If not, then regular NPK fertilizer application should correct the problem.

CALCIUM: Apply lime to bring the pH up to 6.5. If apples are severely and consistently affected, spray the fruit every two weeks with 0.2 per cent solution of calcium nitrate. Use a proprietary tomato feed for tomatoes affected with blossom end rot but pay special attention also to watering.

MAGNESIUM: Scarcely worthwhile but if calcium is deficient too, apply magnesian limestone to the soil.

IRON: Don't use any lime. Apply sequestered iron in the spring at the manufacturers' recommended rate.

MANGANESE: Rarely necessary or worthwhile, but affected plants may quite often be cured by spraying them with 0.15 per cent solution of manganese sulphate.

BORON: Rake in borax at the rate of about 34g per 10 square metres (1oz per 10 square yards) at planting time.

GENERAL: Don't imagine that these deficiences are all common. They aren't. If you routinely use general fertilizers, your plants will usually be alright. Only in certain types of soil or in very wet seasons can problems be expected.

INDEX

Page numbers in *italic* refer
to the illustrations

INDEX

ACKNOWLEDGMENTS

All the photographs reproduced in this book are courtesy of
Professor Stefan Buczacki with the exception of the front cover, main picture
which was supplied by Photos Horticultural

Colour illustrations by Dick Barnard